Are You Listening?

Ralph G. Nichols, PH.D.

Leonard A. Stevens

McGRAW-HILL BOOK COMPANY, INC.

ARE YOU LISTENING?

New York   *Toronto*   *London*

To Carla and the Colonel

Preface

Incredible as it may seem when we think about it, this book, to our knowledge, is the first close analysis ever made of the oldest, the most used, and the most important element of interpersonal communication —*listening*.

Throughout history listening has often been the sole medium of learning. By contrast, reading has served as a primary tool of learning for only a few hundred years, but even during this period it is entirely safe to say that more has been learned through oral than visual communication. And today, to all who take note of what is happening, it is obvious that the relative importance of listening is steadily increasing.

When Shakespeare's *Romeo and Juliet* was televised, some 20,000,000 people heard the performance. And we dare say that of this tremendous audience a large percentage of the people—even those who had previously read the drama—began to understand it for the first time. The Greek tragedy *Oedipus the King* was televised, and in one hour more people heard the play than had heard it in all the drama's combined audiences over the past 2500 years.

For some time we have had more radios than bathtubs. There are 30,000,000 television sets in the United States and more to come. On a Sunday evening between seven and eight over 2,000,000 people are riding along the nation's highways listening to their car radios. If there's a choice between a heater and a radio in an automobile, the typical buyer takes the radio. In the average home in America radio and television sets are heard during almost a third of the waking hours.

The written word is slow compared with the spoken word, a factor that makes listening more and more important in this age of speed. In times of crisis the President of the United States rushes to the microphones, and it is conceivable that every man, woman and child in the country might listen to him as he talks. When matters must be settled in a hurry in today's business, the slow procedures of paperwork are often dropped and people reach for telephones. Even in the normal course of business we find that white-collar workers receive some 40 per cent of their salaries for listening. The world's most important affairs are conducted around conference tables, and at any given moment in a conference, when one person talks the remainder should be listening. We climb aboard great airliners that may take us into clouds so dense that they obscure the wingtips, and as we ride through the murky skies, our lives often depend upon the listening ability of the men on the flight deck.

Compared with the written word, the spoken word has greater persuasive power because, among other reasons, listeners are more vulnerable than readers. Hitler led a literate nation to its downfall, not so much by what he wrote, but mostly by his oral abilities. What we eat, the pills we take, the way we fix our hair, what we wear, how we decorate our homes, the moral codes in which we believe, how we vote, the justice that we deal—all are affected greatly by the way we listen. The most persuasive salesmen do not rely upon writing; they talk. Advertisers find that their messages become most powerful when picked up and passed along by word of mouth. The commercial success of our powerful electronic mass media depends upon the persuasiveness of the spoken word. And the airways and railways are full of people en route to speak personally with other people; the traveling talkers instinctively know that the spoken word can have more effect than the written word.

But if we weigh our educational systems in terms of communication instruction, we find that almost all of the formal attention is given to teaching reading and writing, some is given to speaking and almost none is paid to listening.

The eye has been the favored child in education while the ear has been left to shift for itself—and the neglected ear functions poorly in a world where it is forced to work overtime. Our research shows that on the average we listen at approximately a 25 per cent level of efficiency. This is hardly tolerable in an age when oral presentation carries so large a proportion of the total burden of communication. The time has come to face up to this fact.

Listening is a skill. It can be improved through training and practice, just as can reading, writing and speaking. Listening instruction is presently offered in at least 22 of our leading colleges and universities and in a number of our public and parochial schools. Current interest among educators indicates that within a few years such instruction will spread throughout our entire educational system, becoming a basic part of every modern curriculum.

This book is written to develop the reader's awareness of the importance of listening and to lead him to the kinds of aural experience that make for better understanding of what he hears.

Ralph G. Nichols and Leonard A. Stevens

Contents

Are You Listening?

Chapter 1

The Missing "L" in Learning—Listening

At 8 P.M., October 30, 1938, about six million people across the United States heard the following announcement on their radios:

"The Columbia Broadcasting System and its affiliated stations present Orson Welles and the Mercury Theater of the Air in *The War of the Worlds,* by H. G. Wells."

The announcement was followed by a weather report and dance music. Suddenly the dance music was interrupted with a "flash" news story. "A series of gas explosions has just been noted on the planet Mars," said the announcement. The broadcast went on to report that a meteor had landed near Princeton, New Jersey, killing fifteen hundred persons. Before many minutes, however, the announcer explained that it wasn't a meteor, but a metal cylinder from which poured Martian creatures with death rays to attack the earth.

The program lasted one hour. At the half-hour, two announcements were made indicating that what people were hearing was only a fictitious story. The same sort of an announcement was made at the program's conclusion. And

1

at least 60 per cent of all stations carrying the program interrupted the play to say it was fiction.

But, at their radios that night, there were about a million people who missed these announcements. Only the word "invasion" caught their ears, and it gripped them with fear.

Twenty families on a single block in Newark, New Jersey, rushed from their homes to escape what they thought was a gas raid. Their faces were covered with wet towels and handkerchiefs.

A San Francisco man phoned authorities: "My God, where can I volunteer my services?" he said. "We've got to stop this awful thing."

In Mount Vernon, New York, a man who was considered a hopeless invalid heard the broadcast. With the news of "invasion" he rushed from his home, climbed into an automobile and disappeared.

Warnings and farewells were phoned by mistaken listeners to their friends and relatives all over the country. Telephone lines to radio stations, newspapers, hospitals and police stations were kept busy with people asking about the invasion.

In New York, at one point during the program, Orson Welles and his actors looked up from their microphones to see the studio control room filling up with police. Before long Welles and his colleagues realized that they had caused a panic of national proportions.

The "Invasion from Mars" radio program has been a favorite subject of study for psychologists. At the time, America's nerves were jittery. Munich had occurred only a month before the broadcast date. News flashes about the European crisis were common. The Mercury Theater's simulated flashes with the word "invasion" fell into the pattern of the times, and a million people thought war had suddenly been thrust upon them. Psychologists have used the incident as a case history of how people can panic in a time of crisis.

WE'RE BAD LISTENERS

I look upon the "Invasion from Mars" from another viewpoint. To me the incident is a case history illustrating how poorly millions of Americans listen. Admittedly, the times were ripe for such panic, and the Mercury Theater broadcast was extremely realistic. But it should be noted that the nation's radio sets were being tuned by people who are notoriously bad listeners. The program's announcements carried the information that would have prevented panic. The context of the broadcast itself contained clues that the program was not true. Subsequent research by Princeton University showed that many people who did not panic had put their minds at ease by carefully listening to the story's context. However, the fact remains that about one-sixth of the radio listeners did not use their listening ability in a critical fashion to discover what was really happening.

My field of study for more than a decade—mostly at the University of Minnesota—has been focused upon the art of listening. I began my career as a speech teacher and coach of intercollegiate debating, supplementing my work in speech education with an extensive personal program of speechmaking. My work taught me a great deal about listeners, and eventually my interests shifted from the sending to the receiving side of oral communication.

A person who frequently makes public speeches soon becomes deeply impressed with an important fact: People in general do not know how to listen. They may come to hear you speak, but they are not necessarily good listeners. The burden of making people listen has always been thrown almost entirely upon the speaker. He is given many suggestions for carrying this burden. He may even be advised to perform acrobatics or tell off-color jokes. At any rate, the speaker soon learns that he must engage in an everlasting courtship of his listeners if he wants to be heard.

This recognition of poor listening doesn't confine itself to the field of formal speech. Many businessmen, for example, prefer to bury themselves in paper work rather than depend upon transmitting information from mouth to ear.

A while ago a friend of mine overheard two businessmen talking in the waiting room of the Madison, Wisconsin, airport. The men were discussing a purchase order that was urgently needed from their home office in Chicago.

"Did you let John know how to prepare the order and exactly where to send it?" asked one of the men.

"Yes, this morning," said the other man.

"How? Did you wire him?"

"No, by telephone."

"Good Lord, no!" The man groaned. "Don't ever depend on John getting anything straight verbally. You've got to get it into writing for him, so it will stare him in the face. You better get a wire off right now. Say that you're sending it to confirm your phone conversation."

Such fear of oral communication has caused some companies to set up policies that almost prohibit business from taking place through word-of-mouth. One New York City firm provides every desk with a printed memo pad on the top of which are these bold black letters: DON'T SAY IT! WRITE IT!

Poor listening is one failing that most people recognize

and admit in themselves. When I travel around the country giving speeches on the subject of listening, I find that people readily confess to being poor listeners. Indeed, their confessions are usually open and cheerful. I frequently hear such admissions as these:

"I can sit and look at a person and never hear a word he says."

"My wife is always giving me the devil because I don't pay attention to what she says."

At the same time, I have met few people who really feel that their poor listening habits are an asset. They give lip service to the need for good listening, but they seldom give a moment's thought to what could be done about it.

Behind all of these personal feelings there's a real basis of fact.

For the last several years I have been testing the ability of people to understand and remember what they hear. At the University of Minnesota we have examined the listening ability of several thousand students and of hundreds of business and professional people in adult-education courses. In each case the person tested listened to short talks by various faculty members and was then given a carefully constructed, standard test which was designed to measure the subject's comprehension and retention of the aurally received material.

These extensive tests have led me to this general conclusion: Immediately after the average person has listened to someone talk, he remembers only about half of what he heard—*no matter how carefully he thought he had listened.*

What happens as time passes? My own testing shows—and it has been substantiated by reports of research at Florida State University, Michigan State University and elsewhere—that two months after listening to a person talk, the average listener will remember only about 25 per cent of what was said.

LISTENING IS USED MOST

A number of years ago, the need for better listening came dramatically to the attention of educators. In 1929 they were confronted with the results of an interesting survey which indicated that listening may well be our most important element of personal communication. The survey was made by Paul T. Rankin, who was supervising director of research and adjustment for the Detroit public schools. Rankin had selected 68 adults of different occupations and asked them to keep tabs, every fifteen minutes, of the amount of time they spent talking, reading, writing and listening. The survey was carried on by the 68 people for approximately two months.

The results of Rankin's investigation have kept many educators alert to the need for better listening. He found that on the average, 70 per cent of his subjects' waking day was spent in verbal communication. Also, Rankin learned that of all their verbal communicating time, the 68 adults spent an average of 9 per cent in writing, 16 per cent in reading, 30 per cent in talking and 45 per cent in listening.

Although the survey indicated that we use almost three times as much time listening as reading, little attention was given to training people to listen. In the Detroit public schools Rankin discovered that reading received 52 per cent of the emphasis in classroom instruction, and listening only 8 per cent.

The survey of 68 people by Rankin may mean little if harshly analyzed in terms of scientific research. A research expert might easily prove that, for technical reasons, the accuracy of such a survey may be open to doubt. But regardless of technical merit, Rankin's simple survey may be one of the most important pieces of educational research in several generations.

It pointed up a truth that has been overlooked in our schools from the very beginning. The survey brought us face to face with the fact that for the improvement of personal communication our school curriculums have been seriously out of balance. The eye has occupied the favored position, with the visual skills of reading and writing getting chief attention. Meanwhile, the aural skills of speaking and listening have been kept in the background, improving in a hit-or-miss fashion, if at all. But when we leave school, personal communication most often depends upon the ear. Most of an adult's information is gained through listening. The poorly trained ear works overtime, while the well-trained eye has only a part-time job. The percentage of time spent reading drops off rapidly when school is over for good.

A friend of mine, Ernest H. Ulm, sales manager for the electronics division of Sylvania Electric Products, Inc., decided a while back to see how much he was being paid for listening. As a beginning for his personal survey, Ulm asked his secretary to keep tabs on the time he spent on the telephone. The secretary found that her boss devoted between 70 and 80 per cent of his working day to telephoning and that he spent about half of his telephone time in listening. Ulm was surprised when he translated the little survey into salary terms. His company was paying him 35 to 40 per cent of his salary for listening on the telephone, to say nothing about listening in other situations.

More recently Dr. Donald E. Bird of Stephens College in Missouri made a personal communications survey for the American Dietetic Association. He mailed questionnaires to dieticians in hospitals all over the country and in U.S. territories. The questionnaires were answered and returned by 110 dieticians located in 47 states, Hawaii and the District of Columbia. In one part of the questionnaire, Dr. Bird asked the dieticians to rate reading, writing, speaking and listening in order of their importance on the job. The results:

Reading	4%
Writing	11%
Speaking	22%
Listening	63%

The 110 dieticians estimated that they spent about three times as much time listening on their jobs as they did reading.

From other kinds of studies, there's plenty of evidence to indicate that people are more influenced by what they hear than by what they read.

Several studies have shown that in political elections people receive their information mostly from what they hear. The Survey Research Center of the University of Michigan studied the mediums through which voters received the most political information in the 1952 elections. The researchers found that 27 per cent of the information came from newspapers and magazines, while 58 per cent came from radio and television.

Columbia University's Bureau of Applied Social Research has made impressive surveys to find how people reach their decisions for voting. The results from two of these surveys have already been published. In a study of the 1940 Presidential election the bureau's research workers asked voters in Erie County, Pennsylvania, whether they considered newspapers or radio to be their most important source of information for making their voting decisions. Of those asked, 38 per cent said the radio was their most important source, while 23 per cent gave the credit to newspapers.

In its work on voting, the Columbia Bureau found that "personal influence" was probably the most important factor in determining the decisions of voters. Most of this influence results from what voters hear among their families, fellow workers, neighbors, friends—and even what they overhear in public places.

One restaurant waitress, for example, who was going to vote for Wendell Willkie, switched and voted for President Franklin D. Roosevelt. She was asked why she changed her mind.

"I had done a little newspaper reading against Willkie," she told an interviewer, "but the real reason I changed my mind was from hearsay. So many people don't like Willkie. Many customers in the restaurant said Willkie would be no good."

More recently the Columbia Bureau has found that "personal influence," which depends heavily upon people listening to people, affects the lives of nearly everyone. It will often determine what a woman wears, how she fixes her hair, how she brings up her children and what she feeds her husband.

As we look around we see more and more how much we rely upon the way people listen. Our jury system depends entirely upon the listening ability of the jurors. In every trial by jury we expect twelve men and women to listen to evidence, sometimes running into millions of words, and then decide what is a just verdict.

Possibly you haven't thought of it in this way, but a large percentage of the reports you read in your newspapers depend upon people listening to people. Reporters receive much of their information from oral interviews with their news sources, from speeches and press conferences. If the journalists are to be fair and accurate, they have to be the best of listeners.

Authorities in industry are concluding that sometimes good or bad listening can even make or break a business. They realize that large businesses today are hung together by their communication systems, and industry is spending hundreds of millions of dollars to make these systems work. At the same time many industrialists know that good business communication is a dying cause if the people involved are poor listeners.

Dr. Earl Planty, executive counselor for the pharmaceutical firm of Johnson & Johnson at New Brunswick, New Jersey, says: "By far the most effective method by which executives can tap ideas of subordinates is sympathetic listening in the many day-to-day informal contacts within and outside the work place. There is no full-blown system that will do the job in an easier manner. ..."

FALSE ASSUMPTIONS ABOUT THE EARS

Behind the widespread inability to listen lies what, in my opinion, is a major oversight in our system of classroom instruction. We have focused our attention upon reading, considering it the primary medium by which we learn, and we have practically forgotten the art of listening. About six years are devoted to formal reading instruction in our school systems. Little emphasis is placed on speaking, and almost no attention has been given to the skill of listening. Listening training—if you could possibly call it training—has often consisted of a long series of admonitions extending from the first grade through college: "Pay attention!" "Now get this!" "Open up your ears!" "Listen!"

Certainly our teachers feel the need for good listening. But why have so many years passed without our educators' developing formal methods of teaching students to listen? My conclusion is that we have been faced with at least four false assumptions which have blocked the teaching of listening.

1. We have assumed that listening ability depends largely on intelligence, that "bright" people listen well and "dull" ones listen poorly.

This brings to mind a declaration that we have all heard at one time or another: "You can't tell him anything. He's stupid."

There's no denying that low intelligence has something to do with our ability to listen, but on the other hand, we have tended to exaggerate its importance. A poor listener is not necessarily a stupid person.

To be a good listener we must apply certain skills that have to be learned, either through experience or training. If a person hasn't acquired these listening skills, his ability to understand what he hears will be low. This can happen to people with both high and low levels of intelligence.

One time at the University of Minnesota we ran a series of tests to see if there is a difference between the listening ability of males and females. The females had the higher average intelligence scores, but on the listening tests we found that 95 out of 100 males were better listeners than the females.

On another set of tests we divided up our subjects according to their parents' occupations. Those who came from farm families turned out to be the best listeners. But the farmers' children did not take top honors in intelligence tests given at the same time.

2. We have assumed that listening ability is closely related to hearing acuity, that if a person's ears function correctly he should be a good listener, and that if he's a poor listener he may have something wrong with his ears.

This assumption is proven false by simple statistics. Only 6 per cent or less of the nation's school children are troubled by hearing defects that might impair their ability to learn in the classroom. Tests of ability to understand what is heard show that nearly all children have difficulty in some degree.

3. We have assumed that because everyone gets so much practice in everyday situations of listening, training in this skill is unnecessary. But everyday practice does not make us perfect. We may be practicing faults instead of skills!

Many tests have shown that regardless of age a high percentage of people are still listening as they did in their early school years—and sometimes not as well. Not long ago a large number of schoolteachers cooperated with me to make an informal survey of listening ability. Though unscientific and perhaps not completely valid, the survey's results are typical of those found by more careful testing. I asked each teacher to suddenly interrupt what she was saying during one of her classes and announce: "Time out!" The teacher would then ask the following questions: (1) What were you thinking about? (2) What was I talking about just before I called time out?

In the lower grades, pupils replied to the questions privately with the teachers, who wrote down the results. In the higher grades, the students were asked to write out their answers. None of the students was held responsible for what he answered. The written answers were not signed.

The answers of first-graders showed that 90 per cent were listening to their teachers when time out was called. Over 80 per cent of the second-grade children were listening. The percentages tapered off as the results from higher and higher grades came in. In the junior high grades, only 43.7 per cent of the students were listening. And in high school the average dropped to a low of 28 per cent.

Practice in listening does not make us perfect, unless we are practicing good habits. As with any other skill, listening has its bad habits (the worst of them will be explained in future chapters), and their reinforcement through practice serves to make us poor listeners.

4. We have assumed that learning to read will automatically teach us to listen. While some of the skills attained through reading apply to listening, the assumption is not completely valid. Listening, if you consider it for a moment, is a different activity from reading, and different skills are required. There are two major differences:

Listening is a social activity. The listener is usually confronted by a person talking, and often he is only one of many people listening in the same situation. Reading, however, is usually done alone. The reader can choose his surroundings so as to keep distractions to a minimum. The listener must suffer the distractions that are naturally found when other people are present.

A listener must adjust to the pace of the person talking, but a reader can set his own pace. If the material spoken is difficult to understand and comes at a fast pace, the listener usually cannot slow it down. A reader, however, has the opportunity to slow down, to study and ponder over what is before him. The listener usually hears the words once and they are gone, sometimes for good. The reader can go back to reread until he understands what is written.

Research shows that reading and listening skills do not improve at the same rate when only reading is taught. In general, here's what happens to a student as he goes through school:

The child in the first grade is a better listener than reader. As his schooling progresses a great deal of time is spent on the first "R," reading. In the typical school, however, he will not receive formal training or practice in how to listen.

His ability to read gains a foothold and then begins to improve. As the years go by, his reading ability continues on an upward curve. His listening ability also increases, but it's a losing race. After a few years, probably around the fifth or sixth grade, the youngster's skill at reading is winning the race. He can understand his lessons better by using his eyes than by using his ears.

From this point onward, listening drops farther and farther behind reading. As a fair reader and a bad listener the student is graduated into a society where he will have to listen about three times as much as he reads.

BUT LISTENING CAN BE TAUGHT

The barriers to listening training that have been built up by false assumptions are coming down. Educators are realizing that listening is a skill that can be taught.

One of the most significant factors in the trend to teach listening is found in what we call the "communication movement." Actually this movement began over twenty years ago in a small number of colleges. The freshman year of English, which was always heavily weighted in favor of reading, was replaced by a year of communication training. Such training was a concerted attack to improve students' abilities in all four of their means of personal communication: reading, writing, speaking and listening.

In 1946 the communication movement gained momentum. More than a score of colleges started teaching communication in place of freshman English. By 1951 some 360 colleges had taken up the program. It seems likely that in a few years the vast majority of our schools will present the four-way communication program to their students. Already a large number of colleges and universities offer listening courses in their communication curriculums.

On the St. Paul campus of the University of Minnesota each year the freshman class is tested for listening ability. When the tests are scored, the lowest 20 per cent of the class is given a twelve-week course in listening. At the end of the twelve weeks the entire freshman class is again tested for listening ability. In nearly every class it has been found that the low scorers on the first test have improved their listening ability after twelve weeks' training to the point where they equal or surpass the students who were not required to take the training. Every group of students that has taken listening training has improved at least 25 per cent in its ability to understand the spoken word. Some of the groups have improved as much as 40 per cent.

Also at the University of Minnesota we have given a course in listening for adult-education classes made up mostly of business and professional people. These people have made some of the highest gains in listening ability of any that we've seen. During one period 60 men and women nearly doubled their listening test scores after working together on this skill one night a week for seventeen weeks.

The communication movement—which puts listening on the same level as reading, writing and speaking—is also going into the nation's public and private schools. The interest which has grown in these schools stems importantly from the work of a curriculum commission formed a few years ago by the National Council of the Teachers of English. The commission was assigned the job of studying what could be done to improve language-arts instruction in our schools. In 1953 the first volume of the commission's report was published. The report emphasized the need to give equal weight to listening in conjunction with reading, writing and speaking in classroom instruction.

The recommendation is being put into effect by schoolteachers across the country. The Nashville, Tennessee, public school system, for example, has started a series of listening courses throughout the city's schools from elementary grades to high school. Listening is also taught in the Phoenix, Arizona, and Cincinnati, Ohio, school systems and extensively throughout the state of North Dakota.

How can you possibly teach anyone to listen? In a nation where listening is a forgotten art, this question is not unusual. It is often asked when a person is first told that there are ways of improving ability to hear and understand the spoken word. In future chapters methods for improvement—both for schools and self-improvement—will be explained.

In the meantime, however, you can feel that your listening ability has probably improved already. In most cases, awareness of aural deficiencies is enough by itself to make people do a better listening job on their own.

Chapter 2

Listening's Profits and Pleasures

A man whose acquaintance I made in New England not long ago spent nearly two years on the island of Guam in the Pacific during World War II. He was an Air Force officer and lived during most of his Pacific tour of duty in a quonset hut with several other officers.

"In the next room to me," he said, "there was a fellow from Wisconsin. We spent probably hundreds of hours talking with each other there on Guam. I would have guessed that we discussed nearly everything under the sun, but it turns out that we didn't.

"Not long ago I was in Wisconsin on business and I had a chance to visit my friend from the Air Force. Behind his home I was somewhat surprised to find that he was raising pheasants. He showed me the pheasants and within a few minutes I could see that he knew a great deal about them. What he had to tell me was so interesting that I spent hours asking him about pheasant raising, which, incidentally, was only a hobby for him.

"At one point I asked him if raising pheasants wasn't something new with him, a hobby that he had become interested in after the war.

" 'Oh, no,' said my friend. 'This is something that I've been doing since long before the war.'

" 'But you never told me about it,' I said.

"This surprised my friend, and then, with a laugh, he said, 'I must've figured you wouldn't be interested in hearing about it.' "

The New England man was perceptibly jarred by this remark. He understood himself well enough to know that most of the time he was more likely to be talking than listening, and his experience in Wisconsin made him wonder how many other people had not revealed something about themselves simply because he hadn't cared to listen.

He's not alone in this respect. The majority of us have had the same experience, once or a hundred times, because most people can be classified as "half-listeners." Few people have taken stock of what good listening offers to the person who cares to use his ears.

Before any detailed discussion of the aural processes, let's make at least a partial inventory of how their proper use can profit us. The teacher of listening soon discovers that few people are aware of what they miss by poor listening. To help them become aware of the personal benefits is one of the first steps toward improvement. There are four areas in which doors can be opened by better performance.

1. Broadening knowledge

First of all, opportunity never ceases to knock for anyone who wishes to increase his knowledge or broaden his experience by listening.

At most any moment, your ears have the opportunity of gathering information for you because nearly anyone within hearing distance becomes a potential source of information. The man seated next to you on a train or plane has possibly spent a lifetime becoming an authority on some subject, and the chances are good that, for an interested listener, he will pass on a wealth of pertinent information. A colleague where you work may have a store of experience in the field of your own interests; he is likely to become a free tutor if you only care to listen. A guest who comes for dinner may have been on a trip, and he is certainly willing to tell about it. By listening you may pick up information that cost the man several years' savings to acquire.

In addition to its availability, there are other advantages that go with information received through listening to the people around us.

+ A talker who has wide knowledge of a subject is likely to select his facts to consolidate his information as he speaks in an effort to give you the gist of the subject. For you to do the same kind of consolidating from reading through the breadth of a subject could take weeks or months.

+ Most people, when they talk, learn to watch their listeners' reactions and to use them, consciously or unconsciously, as guides to tailor the spoken word so that it will be more easily comprehended. A talker, for example, will repeat and rephrase what he says if he feels that it will help a listener understand. The same kind of adjustment is not so easily accomplished between a writer and a reader.

+ If a listener still fails to understand what is spoken, he usually has the opportunity of asking on-the-spot questions for clarification. The opportunities for readers to question writers are few indeed.

+ Through listening we can often obtain information that is not written down. Perhaps there hasn't been time to put the information into writing, or there has been no occasion to make the effort.

These are a few of the advantages that listening offers when it is well used as a learning tool. To see how these advantages are put to use, let's take a brief look at a field of work where good listening is crucial. Though essentially considered a writer, a journalist must first of all know how to apply listening ability.

The journalist frequently reports on subjects of great breadth, yet, in his report, a subject must be condensed to only a few thousand words, or even far less. His presentation must also contain the very latest information on a subject with enough background to give the reader a general idea of the whole subject. And for all this work, there's usually a deadline which lies only a few hours, or days at the most, in the future. How does he meet such assignments?

For an explanation, pretend that you, working as a journalist, are told to write three thousand words giving an up-to-the-minute account of what atomic radiation means. You know little about the subject. You are to write for people who know very little about it. You have three days to complete the assignment.

If you follow the working procedure of a good journalist, you will probably go to the nearest person considered an authority on the subject. You will ask him to summarize what he knows about atomic radiation in language that you, as a layman, can understand. The chances are that this authority will oblige, because, after all, you are asking him to talk about his pet subject, one that he may have spent years developing. If he is like most people he will do his best to help you understand his topic—by simplifying his language, by explaining things with parables, by repeating and rephrasing until he can see that you understand.

In the course of his talking he will mentally sift his broad knowledge for pertinent material, a job that might have taken you days or weeks to accomplish in a library. And there's a good chance that your authority will have the latest information on atomic radiation and will pass it along to you. Throughout your interview, if you fail to understand, you have the opportunity to ask questions until things are clear.

This man may lead you to another authority, and the performance can be repeated with him. He may add new facts, recapitulate what the first man said, and further clarify the subject.

By following such a course of action and by listening well, you can be ready to write in a very short time. You will have built a reliable working knowledge of the subject, because your information, to use the vernacular, will have come from "the horse's mouth."

Few of us are journalists, and we may not always have access to all the authorities that journalists can reach. But we can be listeners, and by using the journalist's techniques we have a powerful tool for learning many of the things we need to know. Indeed, here is an area where a degree of selfishness is even appreciated by others. If, by careful listening, you take what other people offer, they will like you for it. And the more you accept the happier will be the person speaking.

2. *Appreciation of the written word*

Several years ago, in a rather odd situation, I ran across another of the benefits offered by the art of listening—and again it's a benefit that many of us neglect.

I had just become a teacher in a small Iowa high school. In this school, William Shakespeare was probably hitting one of the highest peaks of popularity that he has ever attained in an American school. The English Bard's plays and poems were avidly read by a large percentage of the students. Each year several Shakespearian dramas were presented in the school's auditorium, and each play, in terms of attendance, was a smash hit.

Shakespeare's popularity struck me as something close to a miracle, but I soon learned the reason behind the English playwright's reception there in the corn belt.

The English teacher was a good actor, and he enjoyed reading aloud to the students. Shakespeare was not required *reading*. The students were simply asked to listen. The teacher would read a play, changing his voice to fit each of the different parts. At first the readings were a novelty to the youngsters, but slowly they found themselves becoming involved in the plays. They discovered that through listening much of the abstruseness disappeared from Shakespeare's works. Many of the boys and girls developed a deep appreciation for Shakespeare, and they followed up their classwork by reading his dramas on their own. Frequently, they did the reading orally. All of this paved the way for the presentation of Shakespearian dramas in the high-school auditorium. The majority of students attended the performances, and many of them insisted on their parents attending the plays.

What happened to Shakespeare there in Iowa points clearly to one advantage of listening over silent reading. The incident helps prove a point that many educators learn from experience. That is: The enjoyment and appreciation of literature can often be heightened through listening to it. Also, when listening comes first, it often stimulates silent reading of the same material.

These statements have been proven in recent years by

the famous actor, Charles Laughton. During World War II Laughton began reading Shakespeare, Dickens, James Thurber and the Bible aloud to hospitalized servicemen. He soon became so popular as a reader that he traveled America as a one-man show for several years. The show consisted of nothing more than the familiar figure of Charles Laughton lumbering onto the theater's stage with an armful of books from which he read aloud. Laughton was met by enthusiastic audiences and critics who couldn't get enough of his reading. During his performances, Laughton had many experiences that illustrate the effectiveness of listening to literature.

At one hospital Laughton stood before a group of wounded servicemen and suggested that they listen to him read the Bible. His idea was met by protests from a number of servicemen who thought the Bible would be dull. Laughton proceeded anyway, and when he finished there was so much enthusiasm among the men that he was invited back again and again. Laughton's Bible readings led to his making a record album, *Charles Laughton Reads the Bible*, which has been a success.

One time Laughton was reading Shakespeare to a group of teachers at the University of Southern California. One young instructor, after hearing the actor read the "Friends, Romans, countrymen" scene from *Julius Caesar*, insisted that Laughton had edited the Bard's script. Laughton tried to show the man that Shakespeare had not been edited and then asked the instructor why he thought the script had been changed.

"I've read that a dozen times," said the man. "It can't be the same. This is the first time I understood it."

More testimony to the fact that listening adds a new dimension to the written word is found in the phonographic recording business.

Not long ago a customer stepped to a counter in one of

New York's largest record stores and made a request.

"Dylan Thomas?" said the clerk in exasperation. "We can't get enough of him. Why, he moves almost as fast as Toscanini!"

Behind this exclamation lies an interesting tale that bespeaks of the pleasures which people can find in listening to literature.

About 1951 two girls in their early twenties decided to go into a business which would meet what they felt was a need in phonographic recordings. Barbara Cohen and Marianne Roney had met in a Greek class at Hunter College, where they were both majoring in the humanities. After college they worked at different jobs for a few months, but then joined to form a company that would sell records with only spoken words, no music.

In the record world the two girls were laughed at. A few spoken-word records had been made by some of the large record makers, but none of them could be called outstanding commercial successes. The two girls, however, felt that the existing spoken-word records were not presenting the kind of material that could profit most from oral presentation. They intended to record the very best of modern and classical literature, spoken by the living authors of the literature where possible, or by top-notch actors when authors were not available.

The girls named their new firm "Caedmon" after a seventh-century poet. With only a few dollars of capital, the Caedmon girls called on Dylan Thomas, the poet, and Laurence Olivier, the actor. The two men made recordings for the girls, who published 500 records of each man's readings. In one week the thousand records were gone, and surprised record dealers were crying for more. Miss Cohen and Miss Roney knew they were in business.

In four years the Caedmon publishers sold 125,000

copies of the Dylan Thomas recording, and this number, in the eyes of anyone who makes records, is "big." The two girls, after their first success, pursued many of the world's famous writers and signed them up to record their own writings. The girls also hired some of the nation's best actors to record classical literature. Today, Caedmon, located in a loft on Fifth Avenue near Thirtieth Street in New York, is one of the most talked-about businesses in the world of records. In the spoken-word-record field, the Caedmon girls are the stiffest competitors of the nation's largest producers of recordings.

At least six recording companies are supplying the nation with records on which there are only words. At your record store you can now find a wealth of recorded literature. A large part of Shakespeare has been recorded. You can hear Robert Frost reading his poetry as it was recorded in May, 1956, at the poet's home. A reading of "The Rime of the Ancient Mariner" has been a big success on records, selling 20,000 copies within a few months. You can buy a record from which you hear the famous Irish writer Sean O'Casey reading from his own works. The recording was made at the fireside of O'Casey's home in Devon, England, and in the background you can hear the snapping of the fire and the whistle of a distant train. At the rate which producers of spoken-word records now proceed, it won't be long before we can hear all the living writers (those, anyway, who will submit to the recording machine) reading their own words.

This trend of the popularity of the spoken word is looked at over a cold shoulder by people who claim that silent reading should be man's most pleasurable pastime. However, their fears of what may happen to silent reading in face of recorded literature are unwarranted. People listen to a piece of literature from a record and, if they like it, there's a good chance that they will want to read it. The Caedmon publishers receive a large quantity of mail from their listeners and many of the letters ask where the text for spoken-word recordings can be found. Caedmon and several of the other record publishers now include written text with their spoken-word recordings.

Another example of how good listening can lead to good reading is found with a recording made by Dylan Thomas. In searching for something to fill out one of his records, Thomas found a short prose piece that he had written for *Harper's Bazaar* in 1950. It was called "A Child's Christmas in Wales." Thomas recorded the story and it was sold by the thousands. Today the story is considered a classic. Those who listened to "A Child's Christmas in Wales" recognized its literary value and demanded to read it. A book publisher in 1954 printed the story between hard covers and found that it sold very well.

The lately arrived vendors of spoken-word records are not the first to find that good listening can pave the way to reading. Librarians across the country have recognized the fact for a long time. One of the best ways of leading a child to the library bookshelf is by oral storytelling. When children hear stories, their literary appetites are whetted and they return to read.

In the Library School of Pratt Institute, Brooklyn, New York, assistant professor of librarianship Mrs. Ruth Hewitt Hamilton says, "The story hour can be a valuable part of a library program. . . . It enhances the charm of the library as a pleasant and personal place to go. Most important of all it stimulates the imagination, provides the release of laughter, and cultivates an appreciation of the foundations of children's literature."

"The future contribution of storytelling may well surpass all that has gone before," says Mrs. Francis Clarke

Sayers, lecturer in storytelling at the University of California. "In an age when all the world's not a stage but a screen, a picture, a delineation of the obvious object and the obvious symbol for emotion; in an age when the imagination is dulled and stunted by a surfeit of pictures and magazines, textbooks, billboards, buses and newspapers; in an age when every hour of the day and night is filled with shadows of men and women moving fast, talking fast, lest they should lose their Hooper rating—in such an age, the art of the storyteller remains, giving his listeners the space, the time, and the words with which to build in their imaginations the 'topless towers,' 'the stately pleasure domes,' the shapes and sounds none knows nor hears save each mind for itself."

To seek the pleasures of listening to good literature, we don't have to pay to hear a Charles Laughton, or to buy a spoken-word recording, or to send our children to the library story hour. Reading aloud to one another is an art that we can all enjoy with a little practice.

The greatest block to oral reading at home or among friends is something that to my mind is only a misconception. Many of us assume falsely that we lack the voice or the proper diction for reading aloud, and that because of such failings no one would care to listen to us. But this is seldom true. We don't need to be accomplished actors to read aloud and find that others can listen with pleasure. Indeed, the one thing that we should avoid when reading aloud is striving to sound like an actor. With a little practice, oral reading can be made entirely satisfactory. There are only two factors that a reader needs to consider.

First comes an elementary point, but one that is sometimes overlooked. The reader must speak clearly, taking time to articulate the words properly.

Second, the reader must be aware that he is *communi-*

cating the written words to his listeners. To communicate well, he needs an understanding of what the words mean. Sometimes this understanding can come as the oral reading proceeds, but at other times it requires a few minutes' study before the words are spoken.

Today the pleasures of listening to good literature are almost limitless through the simple medium of reading aloud to one another. The very best of literature is now available in low-priced books, rental libraries and public libraries.

So far the possibilities of finding good listening from radio and television have not been mentioned here. Many of the programs, to be sure, do not require a great deal of mental effort. For them, "aural exposure" is all that's required, not what might seriously be termed careful listening. But fortunately there are excellent programs on radio and television from which people can profit and find genuine listening pleasure.

The key to taking advantage of these programs is tied up in the word "selectivity." In this case, being selective is opposed to turning on the radio or television set and letting it blare out come-what-may. There are dramas well worth listening to. There are excellent news programs, commentaries and documentaries. Educational programs are occasionally available—definitely so if there's an educational station within range of your receiving set.

People who have made a study of listening might offer a guide for selecting radio and television programs that will help improve listening ability. We have found that listening is not an easy, passive act if done well. It requires a great deal of effort, as you will see in future chapters. It's only through such effort that we can derive real profit and pleasure from listening. The programs that require mental effort from those who tune in, and the ones that need only "aural exposure," are not hard to choose between.

3. Development of language facility

Through the medium of good listening there's another important way that we can profit, and I have seen it at work as a teacher sitting through or observing hundreds of speech-class sessions.

Where public speaking is taught, the students usually learn through the experience of speaking before their own classes. Each student takes his turn while his colleagues become his audience. While waiting his turn, a student may be required to remain a member of the audience through several hours of speeches. It has always been interesting for me to observe what unguided speech-class audiences do.

Some of the girls knit socks for their boy friends. The knitters often pretend to listen to the speeches, but it is usually obvious that their minds are thinking of those who will wear the socks. Some of the boys simply watch the girls knit. Other students take the opportunity to study. On their laps they hold books or notes to examine during the speechmaking. Many of the students, however, study their own speeches, looking at their speech notes and mentally mouthing the words that they will speak when their turn arrives. And then, of course, there's the exception: the person who listens to the speeches.

In such an audience, who do you think makes the best speaker when his turn comes?

Perhaps you will suspect that it's the fellow who spends his class time reviewing his speech notes and practicing what he is going to say. If so, the answer is wrong.

For any speech teacher the answer is probably easy.

Those who spend their time listening to their colleagues become the better speakers, almost invariably.

Listening is the best way known for improving language facility. As children we automatically become good imitators. The same faculty carries through to adulthood. In a speech class the good listener has the opportunity to hear what makes for good speaking. As a member of the listening audience he can judge for himself, and he can learn what's good and what's bad by the criticisms made of speakers by the instructor. The listener can then imitate that which is good in what he hears.

Those who teach foreign languages have learned in recent years that listening is their most effective tool. For example, here is part of an advertisement printed in a brochure from the Berlitz School of Languages in New York:

"Once upon a time," says the brochure, "when you were very small, you learned a language so easily, so quickly, and so painlessly that you never knew it was happening. That language was English, which was once just as unknown to you as Tibetan is today. But by listening to your parents and imitating them, you learned this language, swiftly, effortlessly and permanently.

"Obviously, the ideal way to acquire more languages with the same speed and ease is to follow that same simple, proven technique .... Berlitz schools ... employ this human, natural system for teaching foreign languages."

Although we learn our native tongue by listening to our parents, few of us are aware of the ways we change our language through listening to others as life goes on.

We are all like the country boy who left the farm for the city and then returned to be accused of talking like a city slicker. That city talk rubs off onto a fellow from the country the more he listens to it.

By making a frequent effort to hear the best of speech,

a person has the opportunity to learn about the structure of good language and grammar. He can improve his own use of voice. And his vocabulary is almost certain to improve. When unfamiliar words are heard, their meanings are frequently learned from the context in which they are set. And vocabulary through listening comes with a built-in pronunciation guide that works more easily and efficiently than any found in a dictionary.

But again it should be stressed that these advantages are found only after an effort is made to associate with good speech—by listening to friends who speak well, by good radio and television listening, by attending lectures that have value, by listening to the sermon in church—they all offer the opportunity for language improvement. On the other hand, it is well to remember that language facility can retrogress if we continually listen to poor speech and do not make a frequent effort to listen to talkers who can upgrade our language.

4. Therapeutic value

There's one more major profit to be found in listening to people talk that is well worth considering. We've all seen it operate in the use of the child's bedtime story. The child listens and he slowly relaxes, dropping the day's cares until he goes to sleep.

In his classrooms at the Delaware State Society for Mental Hygiene, Col. H. Edmund Bullis has used good listening to advantage. Students in the classes often hear "stimulus stories" related by the teacher. After listening to a story, the students discuss it and tell of their own related experiences, or opinions. This simple procedure has sometimes produced outstanding results, stimulating oral expression, releasing tensions, and changing attitudes and behavior patterns. With this kind of classroom activity, apathetic, unresponsive or recalcitrant students have often shown interest that couldn't be stirred up in other ways.

In the adult world the therapeutic value of listening has been associated mostly with music. However, appreciative listening to stories, poetry, drama, good conversation and the like also can help us relax, to put aside personal worries and cares. This is not to intimate that good listening is a panacea for deep-seated psychological disturbances, but it can serve as a relaxing agent against our lesser worries.

In this chapter an effort has been made to point up some of the major profits and pleasures of listening. There are no secret formulas for taking advantage of what good listening has to offer. If there's anything even approaching a formula it can be said in one word: "awareness." If each person would simply make an accounting of what he can enjoy and how he can profit from the art of listening, he would have taken a giant step in the realm of self-improvement.

Chapter 3

How Listening Controls Talking

Each spring many of the faculty members at the University of Minnesota travel to outlying high schools to serve as commencement speakers for high-school graduations. At one such event I underwent the most nerve-wracking experience of my public-speaking career.

On a lovely spring evening I drove to a small town in northern Minnesota. I entered the local auditorium, met the high-school officials and took my seat on the platform. The audience, as usual at such functions, was full of fathers, mothers, grandfathers, grandmothers, uncles, aunts and assorted cousins. There were several hundred people in the auditorium.

After speeches by members of the graduating class, I was introduced. I had hardly finished my speech's introduction when a child began to cry. This was not new for graduation, so I continued without being particularly upset. Soon the wails of a second child joined those of the first. Then a little boy started running up and down the aisle and no one stopped him. The audience was distracted. A second lad started a pursuit of the first youngster in the aisle. The old wooden seats in the auditorium creaked as people twisted around to see what was happening.

Suddenly I was in the worst situation imaginable for a public speaker. I had no listeners. My mouth dried out and it was hard to talk. I ran through all of the techniques I had learned and practiced in the past to regain my audience's attention. I tried projecting my voice more. It didn't work. I tried being humorous, but there was no laughter. I walked briskly across the stage, and looked hard at the chief area of disturbance. It was no use.

In a desperate effort to keep from going to pieces, I tried one last technique that I had learned long ago. I scanned my audience for a single person who was listening. Finally I found him. He was an old gentleman seated in a row near the front. He was looking at me, nodding his head and smiling. I forgot the bedlam around the man and concentrated on him. He was a wonderful audience. My mouth stopped being dry. Slowly I pulled my speech back together and proceeded to the end of it feeling much better. The old man followed me, responding to every sentence, and apparently approving every point being made.

At the end of the exercises I wanted to escape, but the school superintendent insisted that I stay for refreshments. While having coffee, I noticed my one-man audience standing at the side of the room. He bowed and smiled when I looked his way.

"That man over there," I said to the superintendent. "I noticed him while I was speaking. I would like to meet him."

"Well, yes, I'll try to introduce you," said the superintendent, "but it may be a little difficult. You see, the poor old fellow is stone deaf."

The statement shook me. But then I realized that the

man, regardless of his deafness, had been my savior during the graduation exercises. He had helped me to restore the self-confidence that every speaker must have and which he acquires only when he knows that he is communicating to his audience. Perhaps the deaf man could read lips; I still don't know. Anyway, I walked over to him, shook his hand, and tried to show gratification for the attention he had paid to me.

LISTENERS HELP US TALK

My experience there in northern Minnesota is a specific instance that illustrates a very important truth about human nature: We all crave good listeners.

The public speaker—as illustrated above—must feel that he has listeners or he is licked from the start.

An actor's performances rise and fall according to how well his audiences pay attention.

In a survey of industrial executives' wives, the editors of *Fortune* magazine found that the wives considered "listening to their husbands" as their number-one duty.

A woman in Georgia recently made the following statement upon learning that we teach listening at the University of Minnesota: "Why, that's not new, is it? My mother taught my sisters and me to listen. She understood that women who listen well are attractive to men."

Social caseworkers learn that listening is one of their most valuable tools. They find that personal problems are often relieved if people can only find someone to understand what they have to say about their problems.

There are some medical doctors, with excellent "bedside manners," who are patronized more because they take time to listen than because they are good physicians.

Through attentive and sympathetic listening, psychiatrists are able to bring forth the deepest secrets of a person's mind.

Opposition can often be changed to support by the art of listening. In his 1956 Presidential campaign Adlai Stevenson prefaced his speaking campaign with a listening campaign. When he was nominated in August, there was still opposition to Stevenson within his own party throughout the country. Stevenson traveled from one region to another and met with party officials. At the meetings he talked little and listened a lot. The newspapers reported that those party officials who had been hostile to Stevenson often left the meetings ready to give him their full support.

In one of his biographies, it was said that Calvin Coolidge "was Northampton's champion listener: listened his way into all the offices the town would give him."

WHY THE LISTENING MUST HAVE QUALITY

Although the human demand to be heard may profit the person who can fulfill the need, the dividends are paid only to those offering listening ability that has quality. Sporadic or half-attentive listening is easily detected by the person who is talking.

Nearly all of us have unconsciously developed a special set of senses that, in effect, measure the way people listen when we talk to them. In public speaking we call the process "circuit response," and each speaker attempts to derive positive benefit from this well-known phenomenon. Circuit response is also at work when just one person talks to another. It operates something like this:

As he speaks, the talker's words go out to the listener, and simultaneously the talker expects a reaction to bounce back from the listener. Sometimes the reaction returns in the form of words or even grunts. The listener may only say, "I see," "Oh, yes," or simply, "Hmm." Or the reaction may be negative, with "Oh, no," "How's that?" or another "Hmm" that, according to its tone, indicates misunderstanding or dissent.

But these are the simple reactions. Most of the time the talker's words bring reactions that are only fleeting visual cues. The listener's face may brighten up just slightly to show he understands and approves. The listener looks away from the talker; something is wrong. He looks the talker straight in the eye; things are better. He smiles, nods his head or moves forward ever so slightly and the talker learns that his words are being received well. On the other hand, the listener may screw up his face, scowl, scratch his head, shake his head, or loosen his collar, and the talker feels that his words are not having the right effect. There are hundreds of visual cues—some almost invisible to the human eye—that convey meaning from listener to talker.

And then there's one important reaction that is neither visual nor oral. It is silence, of which there are several brands. There's a cold, chilling brand of silence. There's a demanding kind of silence that says, "Okay, I'm listening so try to tell me something." And there's a warm, receptive quality in some forms of silence that connotes understanding and a desire to hear more. Or silence may simply be neutral, leaving the door open for the talker to proceed, but not giving him much encouragement.

From all such reactions a talker takes his bearings. If the reactions are good they have the effect of loosening him up, of allowing him to think and talk freely. If the reactions are negative the road is rough for the person talking. He automatically struggles to overcome the bad reactions, to change them in his favor. If the reactions are completely bad, they may cause the person to stop talking, and communication ends.

This business of circuit response, of a return reaction when we speak, is more important to our talking effectively than most of us realize. People who work in radio or television sometimes fail to learn this fact.

Most any evening at home, if you have a television set, you can witness one or several people speaking—and finding it a struggle—without benefit of circuit response. Watch some of the announcers, especially those giving commercials. There, for all intents and purposes, they stand in your living room, but few speak accordingly. Many announcers talk in the manner of circus barkers. Often they sound like desperate men trying to hammer some simple-minded message across your parlor. If they came to your home in person they wouldn't think of talking in the same way. They would automatically respond to your feelings and keep their voices down. But our otherwise amazing world of electronics still hasn't made provisions for television listeners to respond immediately to announcers. The man in the studio talks without immediate guidance from his listeners. As a result, announcers often strain harder and harder to put themselves across. This indictment, of course, does not apply to all announcers. The better ones, in deference to the listener, learn to talk as if they were actually in your living room.

RESPONSIBILITY MUST BE SHARED

As you may have noted already, the responsibility for taking advantage of circuit response in our culture is assigned to the talker alone. The good public speaker, for instance, works hard "to get a feeling" for his audience.

He speaks, notes the reaction from his audience and then adjusts his speaking to make matters easier for those who listen. The traditional idea has been that "If you want listeners you must court them as you would a desirable but fickle woman."

In the comparatively new field of listening we cannot accept such a premise. We feel that the listener must share the responsibility for the use of circuit response to improve personal communication. The good listener, we have discovered, produces the kinds of reactions that help the talker, that make it easier for him to bring out what he has on his mind. Furthermore, our studies show that good listeners, as is the case with good speakers, take advantage of the circuit response phenomenon to improve communication.

By the way we respond to people when we listen, we actually exercise a large degree of control over the amount we shall learn through our ears. Sometimes by little more than the lifting of an eyebrow we can either shut off the opportunity to learn, or we can open the doors wide to the possibilities of gaining knowledge through listening. Such reactions are not even on a conscious level with many people. But the fact constitutes no reason for saying that we can't become conscious of many listening reactions, and thereby control them so that they work in our favor. Let's look at an example of what can happen when a person doesn't control his reactions to a person talking.

Not long ago, a colleague of mine at a Midwestern university was hired by the U.S. Army to conduct classes on human relations. On this subject he has a great many ideas worth hearing. The professor was sent to a large Army post to talk to the staff officers. Arriving at the Army post, he was well prepared to present what he felt would be important and useful information for the officers. But he came away knowing that he had given only a small measure of what he had intended to give.

At the post he entered a conference room where the officers were seated around a large table. Among the officers sat the post's commandant, a full colonel. The professor started his talk by telling a story. The story might be considered "off-color" by some people but the professor felt that in a male audience no one would mind. All the officers laughed at the story, except for one man, the commandant. While the other officers were laughing, the professor caught a glimpse of the unsmiling colonel, but for the moment he disregarded the incident and began talking about human relations.

However, as he talked, he couldn't take his eyes off the colonel. Something was wrong—so it seemed to the professor. The colonel seldom looked up. Frequently he massaged his brow with the finger tips of his right hand and occasionally he ran his fingers through his thinning hair. Now and then he used a pencil and paper, but the professor could see that the colonel wasn't taking notes. He was doodling.

The professor became extremely nervous and lost track of what he had intended to say. After the class the professor, reviewing his notes, realized that he had even left out some of his most important points. He was embarrassed with the way he had conducted the class.

Where does the responsibility for this debacle lie?

According to most precepts of public speaking, the professor is to blame because it was his responsibility to grasp the audience's attention, including the commandant's, and hammer across his ideas. But the professor has proven many times that he is a good public speaker. Then why didn't he give a speech equal to what he had intended?

Actually, I feel that the colonel is largely to blame for

this failure. He effectively turned the conference room into a refrigerator, in which few men could talk well.

Perhaps the colonel didn't like the professor's opening joke, decided that it was indicative of what was to come and proceeded not to listen. Or it could be that the colonel had other problems on his mind which superseded listening.

Whatever the reasons were for the colonel's inattentiveness, many good ideas were lost to the entire group of officers.

Everyone has had similar experiences, and not necessarily as a public speaker. You may want to tell your boss something you feel is extremely important for him to know. You walk into his office and begin to talk. His attention wanders. He opens his mail as you struggle through what you have to say. He takes time out for a phone call. Inside you, something dies. You have a tremendous desire to escape. As a result, you cut things short and withdraw. The boss thinks you're a pain in the neck for wasting his time and will never realize that perhaps something he should have heard won't be uttered in his presence.

Most of us have been guilty of the same thing at one time or another. Too often we fail to realize that our listening reactions can make or break the person talking to us. We fail to realize that through the picture which we present to people who are talking to us we can sometimes shut off the flow of information.

WHEN SELFISHNESS IS DESIRABLE

But what are these listening reactions that help people to talk freely, to open up and give us everything that's there?

Most of the time the reactions are hard to pin down.

But several of them have already been mentioned. For example, when we look a person in the eye it tells him that we're interested, that he should go on and say what he wants to say. Or we may simply sit up straight, appearing alert. Or occasionally we will move toward the talker ever so slightly.

But these and the many other reactions that a talker observes in a listener cannot be produced artificially. They're not mannerisms that we can practice and then turn on whenever we think they're needed.

Actually, all the reactions, good or bad, in the listening situation are symptoms of the human attitudes behind them. If we have the right attitudes toward a person talking, the visible reactions will take care of themselves.

An attitude that can produce good listener reactions is one of *enlightened self-interest*. We need not allow any vague notion of selflessness to enter the picture. As listeners we can be as selfish, grasping, greedy, practical-minded and avaricious as we like. The more we take from the speaker through listening, the more he will give.

In future chapters there will be many specific suggestions to help you become a better listener. These suggestions, when followed, will also help form the attitudes that in turn produce the listening reactions which enhance oral communication.

WHO LEARNS BY LISTENING?

But before turning to these chapters, there is a major concept of learning by listening that should be read and pondered. It may help you build awareness of the responsibilities a listener has to a talker when listening is important as a medium for learning.

Learning while listening is inside action on the part of the listener.

The talker cannot learn for the listener. "Telling" doesn't equate with teaching, and "getting told" certainly doesn't equate with learning. Learning is essentially an expansion and refinement of a person's apperceptive mass—that sum total of all the thoughts, feelings, emotions, experiences, facts and ideas one has previously accumulated. Learning takes place when this mass is altered, modified, rearranged, refined or expanded. The person talking cannot do this for the listener. The talker can supply some of the materials for learning, but action taken on the materials must occur inside the listener.

Chapter 4

If Only Someone Would Listen

All of us are frequently motivated by a strong human need to talk to someone who will listen to us.

This struggle for listeners was dramatically illustrated a few years ago in a short story written by John O'Hara. It was called *The Man Who Had to Talk to Somebody.* The story's main character, Williams, worked in an office with the story's author. Occasionally he would take the author out to lunch. During luncheon Williams would remain silent for a long time, and then he would start to tell about his past life, a tragic one. At successive luncheons Williams would talk about the same things from his past, over and over.

"Williams," says O'Hara, "always had to have somebody to talk to when he really wanted to talk, and it didn't seem to make much difference who it was."

Later, Williams was fired. "I am sure I'll never see him again," says O'Hara, "but wherever he is he is probably still taking strangers out to lunch and telling them just the things he told me."

Williams is not an unusual character. The world is full of people like *The Man Who Had to Talk to Somebody.* Perhaps they are troubled, they have problems to solve, or they have nothing special on their minds—they only want to talk to somebody. We all experience the same feeling. It is so good to be able to talk to somebody who will listen. Not that we necessarily have any information to communicate. Nor do we want advice or solutions for the problems we may relate. But we do have a strong desire to be heard, and if someone will sit still and listen we come away feeling that we got something off our chests; that an emotional unburdening took place.

The recognition of this need for listeners is certainly not new. Some 4,400 years ago, Ptahhotep, one of the pharaohs, instructed the viziers and officers of his staff as follows: "An official who must listen to the pleas of clients should listen patiently and without rancor, because a petitioner wants attention to what he says even more than the accomplishing of that for which he came."

The recognition of what lies behind this need for listeners is comparatively new. An understanding of what happens when a person talks and another listens is found at the foundations of today's pyschotherapy. The psychiatrist's most important tool is listening. And "nondirective counseling," now practiced more and more widely throughout business and industry, depends upon persons trained to listen quietly and objectively.

It is not the purpose of this book to discuss lengthily the facets of psychotherapy, and by no means to suggest that we can all become amateur psychotherapists among our friends simply by listening to them. However, many of us do not understand why we are needed as listeners when someone feels he has to talk to get something off his mind. A fairly simple understanding of this need may help to produce the kind of listening that is required.

HE MUST TALK WITH HIMSELF

As you may know, each of us is psychologically constructed in two parts. In effect, we are two persons within one. There's a surface part, the one that a person is aware of in his conscious thoughts. And there is a subsurface part within each person described as "repressed," or "subconscious." The surface part is used for conscious control of what a person says and does. The subsurface part also plays an important role, causing the individual to say or do things more or less unconsciously.

Frequently the two forces within one human being fail to agree, and the person finds himself in trouble. He is torn between what he thinks on the conscious level and what his subconscious mind tells him. You might say that he has two bosses. When he starts to say something, both bosses give orders. What he says, therefore, often comes out distorted. He is not saying what he really means, nor can he always fully understand what he says. With such a situation the person finds it difficult to communicate with other people. Under these conditions he is said to be emotionally maladjusted, or "neurotic."

When there's a conflict between two people, they can sometimes settle their differences by communication with each other. They talk things over until there's a meeting of minds. When there are conflicts between the two levels of a person's mind, communication is also needed to settle the differences. In short, the conscious part of the mind must learn what goes on in the subconscious part in order to bring it under control. This form of communication is the hardest of all. It requires a degree of personal insight that few people have.

However, there is a way that we can communicate with ourselves, but it requires the help of another individual— a listener, and a very good one. If we find such a listener— and they are hard to find—he, in a sense, becomes a mirror that throws back a reflection of ourselves. The listener hears our words but, what is more important, we hear ourselves talking. If the listener remains active, but silent, giving us a chance to talk freely, thoughts from both the conscious and subconscious levels of our brain are put into words. As a result we have the opportunity to hear both parts of our brain speaking. Many times this results in the self-communication we have been seeking.

Let's see how all this works in an actual case.

A number of years ago an associate of mine was teaching a friend to drive an automobile. During one of the lessons the student driver, panic-stricken, pushed the accelerator to the floor and let go of the steering wheel. The car, out of control, went over a bank and struck a large rock. No one was hurt, but both people were thoroughly frightened.

For the next ten years my associate experienced a recurring nightmare in which he dreamed of the accident. Night after night he would leap up from his sleep thinking that he was riding in a car that was out of control.

During this period the man thought the nightmare was caused by fear resulting from the accident. Before going to bed he often would try to talk himself out of the fear. But as well as he thought he understood the nightmare's cause, he couldn't get rid of the bad dream.

In New York City he visited a psychiatrist and explained the problem. The doctor told him that probably the acci-

dent was not the real cause of the nightmare; that undoubtedly there was a deeper source of trouble lying in
his subconscious mind. If this could be brought to light,
said the psychiatrist, the nightmare would probably disappear because the man's conscious mind could then cope
with the problem. The psychiatrist offered to help the man
on this specific trouble.

For a number of hours spaced a week apart the man with
the nightmare visited the psychiatrist. The psychiatrist
asked him to tell about his past life. The doctor wanted
to hear all the thoughts that the man associated with the
nightmare and with other dreams that he could remember.
During each session the psychiatrist, seated across a desk
from his patient, listened patiently and understandingly.

After many weeks a remarkable thing happened to the
patient. "During one or two of the sessions," he says, "the
real reason for the nightmare slowly dawned upon me. For
weeks I had frequently mentioned the strong sway that my
father held over me. He was very much against my leaving
home when I was ready for college. It was his desire that
I remain at home and follow the kind of life he had led,
and it didn't include college.

"But against his wishes I left home. Years later I experienced fear when I felt I had disobeyed my father. I
was afraid that some superior insight might have told him
that in the world away from home I wouldn't be able to
control my life. Here, I slowly realized, was a situation
comparable to the automobile accident. The fear of an
out-of-control automobile was similar to the fear of my life
being out of control. Possibly, I thought, the accident
serves as only a symbol for this deeper feeling. The psychiatrist encouraged me to talk more about this feeling
and it became clearer and clearer in my mind. At the same

time the nightmare went away and it is now a thing of the past."

Here is a case where the listener, in the person of the psychiatrist, allowed the talker to communicate within himself, a thing he had never been able to do by himself. In a very real sense, the man heard his subconscious mind speaking and it told him what lay below the surface to cause the nightmare. Once this communication had occurred the man could cope with the problem on the conscious level and the nightmare ended.

WE ARE ALL SOUNDING BOARDS

Very few people go to psychiatrists with their problems. But many people take their troubles to close friends and relatives. We cannot, as laymen, possibly offer our friends the help that a good psychiatrist gives to a patient. But there's no reason that we can't become helpful listeners. Good listening in such cases can do no harm; it may do some good.

Dr. Elton Mayo of Harvard University says: "One friend, one person who is truly understanding, who takes the trouble to listen to us as we consider our problems, can change our whole outlook on the world."

Dr. Florence Hollis, professor of social work at Columbia University, puts it this way: "When a person knows that he has a good listener to talk to, he'll share his thoughts more fully, which, in turn, makes it easier for the caseworker to help him with his problems. And, moreover, as he talks, the person needing help often finds a good solution to his problems himself."

This helpful kind of listening is most clearly described by the term "nondirective." The word refers to the reaction that a listener should present to a talker who is trying to discuss his own problems. Another way of putting it is to say that the listener makes an effort to understand what is said, but he refrains from giving any directions.

And here we hit upon the major failing of most of us when we are called upon to listen to a person who simply needs to talk. Many times we do not understand the role we are being called upon to play. We feel that we are being asked to offer advice or a good solution to the talker's problems. The moment we start giving the advice, our listening loses its nondirective quality and also its effectiveness.

The good nondirective listener realizes that his role is that of a sounding board. The talker really doesn't want advice. He wants a good reason to talk freely so that he can listen to his own thoughts as they are put into words. With this opportunity to hear both sides of himself speak, he may be able to furnish his own advice or problem solutions.

In brief, the good nondirective listener accepts what is said, tries hard to understand it, and above all, *makes no evaluative judgments.*

Dr. Carl Rogers, the well-known psychologist, put it this way: "If I can listen to what he tells me, if I can understand how it seems to him, if I can sense the emotional flavor which it has for him, then I will be releasing potent forces of change within him.

"Again, if I can really understand how he hates his father, or hates the company, or hates Communists—if I can catch the flavor of his fear of insanity, or his fear of atom bombs or of Russia—it will be the greatest help to him in altering those hatreds and fears and in establishing realistic and harmonious relationships with the very people and situations toward which he has felt hatred and fear.

We know from our research that such empathic understanding—understanding *with* a person, not *about* him—is such an effective approach that it can bring about major changes in personality."

If you would like to find out for yourself how difficult it is to listen without making evaluative judgments, try a little experiment that has been suggested by Dr. Rogers.

The next time you find yourself in a heated discussion with your family or friends, ask that the following rule be put into effect for a time:

"Each person can speak up for himself only *after* he has first restated the ideas and feelings of the previous speaker accurately and to the speaker's satisfaction."

"You see what this would mean," says Dr. Rogers. "It would simply mean that before presenting your own point of view, it would be necessary for you to achieve the other speaker's frame of reference—to understand his thoughts and feelings so well that you could summarize them for him. Sounds simple, doesn't it? But if you try it, you will discover that it is one of the most difficult things you have ever tried to do. However, once you have been able to see the other's point of view, your own comments will have to be drastically revised. You will also find the emotion going out of the discussion, the differences being reduced, and those differences which remain being of a rational and understandable sort."

LISTENING TAKES COURAGE

Why is the seemingly simple act of nondirective listening so difficult to accomplish? The best answer probably lies in the fact that such listening requires a kind of courage that few of us have ever mustered.

Whenever we listen thoroughly to another person's ideas

we open ourselves up to the possibility that some of our own ideas are wrong. Most of us fight change, especially when it has to do with altering thoughts that may have been with us since childhood. Therefore, when we listen, something from inside makes us want to fight the change in our thinking that might be brought about by what we hear. "Hold on there," we are urged to say. "You must be wrong. That isn't the way I think. And you're not going to change my mind. I won't allow it. Now you listen to me."

To face up to the possibility of changing our minds requires courage. Without it nondirective listening is all but impossible. Lack of courage prevents us from opening our ears to whatever may be said, from trying sympathetically to understand the other person's point of view.

There is no exact formula for the kind of listening that can help people when they feel the very human desire to be heard. It depends too much on an attitude that must come from inside the listener. No one can spell out a method by which you can become sympathetic and understanding to another person's point of view.

The foregoing discussion of listening, if it is to be valuable, will have built awareness of the role we should play as listeners when meeting the widespread human need to be heard. But awareness by itself is not enough. It can only serve as the reason behind the desire to form listening attitudes that are valuable to people who need to talk. The development of the attitudes is very much up to the listener himself.

The following six admonitions may be of value to you in forming the attitudes required for nondirective listening. Some of them are symptoms of good listening; some are causes. All may serve very well as guides which will help when the need for nondirective listening arises.

1. Take time to listen

Whenever you sense that someone is troubled, about to "blow his stack," or needs to talk, give him your time if at all possible. Though it may seem like a waste of time to you, it seldom is. If by listening you can help him clear his mind, it will also help clarify communication between you and the person talking. Also, there may come a time when you need a listener, and it is a fact that one good listener has little difficulty finding another one.

2. Be attentive

If a violent tirade is launched, your best contribution will be to let it flow uninterrupted until it is exhausted. Make every mental effort possible to understand what is said. Try to put yourself in the talker's place in respect to what he says.

3. Employ three kinds of verbal reactions only

As the talker proceeds the listener may employ what has been called a series of "eloquent and encouraging grunts": "Hmmm," "Uh-huh," "Oh," or "I see."

If the talker pauses momentarily, the listener should remain silent, perhaps continuing to nod his head indicating understanding, until speech starts again.

If the talker becomes wild and unreasonable, the listener should restate what has just been said, putting it in the form of a question. Examples of such restatements might be: "You really think, then, that all middlemen are dishonest?" Or, "You believe your mother-in-law is deliberately trying to ruin your marriage?"

4. Never probe for additional facts

There's a distinct difference between willingness to listen and curious inquisitiveness designed to obtain information. In the nondirective listening situation the latter must be avoided. Your purpose is not that of obtaining information for yourself.

5. Never evaluate what has been said

You should at all costs to your own feelings refrain from passing moral judgment upon what is heard. In no case should you give the talker advice—even if he requests advice.

6. Never lose faith in the ability of the talker to solve his own problems

Remember that, as the talker speaks, you are witnessing an amazing human phenomenon. He is really talking things over with himself. If you refrain from speaking up to inject yourself into his conversation, the chances are fairly good that the talker will work things out for himself.

Chapter 5

Do You Know How People Talk?

On November 14, 1956, William H. Lawrence, a reporter for *The New York Times,* asked President Eisenhower the following question at a news conference:

"Mr. President, in view of the voters' decision to continue split government, that is, a Democratic Congress and a Republican executive, do you regard the election returns as a mandate to push forward with the program that you have had to re-examine it or to—"

It appears that Lawrence's question at the end became slightly befuddled. But it didn't confuse the President, for he immediately gave an answer. Here are his exact words:

"Well, Mr. Lawrence, I think if I didn't believe that this was somewhat of a mandate to me to push forward with, what I have been trying to tell the United Nations —to the United States, is my policy, my beliefs, my convictions and a program, that then I would be arrogating to myself a tremendous personal magnetism and standing that probably—that probably would make me about as egotistical as any man in the world. If they don't approve what I stand for I would not understand why they voted for me."

And now the President of the United States is caught up

in what reads like a real tongue twister. What's wrong? Can't these two men talk straight?

Of course they can. The print on this page has been unfair to them. You have *read* some words that were really meant to be heard. But if you had been at the press conference you probably wouldn't have had any difficulty understanding the President and Mr. Lawrence. As they spoke, both men undoubtedly used a number of gestures and variations of voice to accompany the sentences that seem so jumbled when you read them.

The President's statement, for example, may have been greatly clarified by a simple shake of his head and change in the rate of speed at which he spoke four words. Right after the words "United Nations," he probably shook his head slightly from side to side, and then quickly spoke the words "to the United States." The head shaking and change of pace would have had the effect of saying, "I made a mistake. I didn't mean United Nations. I mean United States." With this correction, even though it didn't require a single spoken word, the President's answer to the reporter becomes quite clear. Other gestures and voice variations could have made the entire statement sound smooth and completely understandable.

LISTENING IS NOT READING

The press-conference incident is cited to dramatize an important listening factor of which many of us are not aware. It is this:

"Listening requires different skills from reading because the spoken word is not communicated in the same manner as the written word."

At first thought, this may seem pretty elementary.

Nevertheless, it is a truth that has been overlooked in our culture. The failure to see the differences between reading and listening skills helps to create a serious false assumption: that if we learn to read, we automatically learn to listen.

To lay a foundation for listening improvement, let's look at some of the things that make the skill of listening different from that of reading.

In the third century B.C. the Greek philosopher Aristotle said: "It should be observed that each kind of rhetoric has its own appropriate style. The style of written prose is not that of spoken oratory.... Both written and spoken have to be known."

Like Aristotle, people concerned with speaking and writing have been aware that there are differences between the speaker's and the writer's language. At the University of Wisconsin, Professor of Speech Gladys L. Borchers did some research to determine the differences between written and oral style. From all the published advice available about the two styles, Dr. Borchers decided that there could be at least eighteen "rules or suggestions" for oral language.

1. In oral style there is a greater variety of sentence length than in written style.
2. There should be greater variety in sentence structure in oral style.
3. Sentences are less involved in structure in oral style.
4. Personal pronouns "I," "we," and "you" are more numerous in oral than written style.
5. Oral style requires more careful adaptation to the speaker.

6. Oral style requires more careful adaptation to the audience.
7. Oral style requires more careful adaptation to the occasion.
8. Oral style requires more careful adaptation to the subject matter.
9. Fragmentary sentences may be used in oral style.
10. Slang may be used in oral style.
11. Contractions are used more often in oral style.
12. Oral style is more euphonious.
13. Indigenous language should be more predominant in oral style.
14. Repetition is more necessary in oral style.
15. Concrete words should be used more often in oral style.
16. Effusive style or copiousness is more predominant in oral style.
17. Vehement style is more predominant in oral style.
18. The rhythm of oral style is different from the rhythm of written style.

These "rules or suggestions" may seem at first to contradict almost all you have learned in English classes from the first grade through high school or college. They are certainly not the rules for the structuring of good English as most of us have learned it. How could they possibly help anyone become a polished orator?

Actually those eighteen statements are reasonably accurate observations of how people compose their language when they talk as opposed to when they write. They give a fairly good picture of what happens to our language as we talk "off the cuff"—which means: thinking, putting the thoughts into words and communicating them orally, all of which is accomplished almost simultaneously.

But merely to look at the flow of words does not complete the picture of how people talk. There's another side to the picture that has to be considered if a person is to listen well. It's the "nonverbal" side of personal communication.

The French writer Victor Hugo said, "When a woman is speaking to you, listen to what she says with her eyes."

Victor Hugo was talking about what is now fancifully labeled "nonverbal communication."

When people talk, the words they utter are only a part of their effort to communicate. With the words come gestures from the talker's hands and from nearly every muscle in his body. Even the temperature of a person's body, as it shows in the color of his face or the moisture in the palms of his hands, says something about what he is putting into words or about the silence he maintains.

"Self-betrayal oozes from all our pores," said Sigmund Freud.

The pitch and timbre of a person's voice; the way he pauses between words; the rhythm with which the words flow from his mouth; oddities in pronunciation; the speed at which words are spoken—all of these things have something to say, over and above that which is being communicated by words alone.

Erle Stanley Gardner, the mystery writer, wrote the following in *Vogue* magazine recently:

"Voices," said Gardner, "betray other thoughts and emotions. The average man has not trained his ears to the fine nuances of sound so that he can appreciate these things. Animals have this ability. Your dog, with his delicately attuned ears, can tell so much about your emotions and thoughts from the simple sound of your voice that if he could speak to tell you what he has learned you'd be astounded. As it is, the dog shows by his actions something of what he has learned from listening to the tone of your voice.

"For many years," Gardner continues, "I was in partnership with an attorney who had been an expert court reporter; he had reported some famous cases and many important legislative inquiries.

"In those cases, and particularly in the legislative hearings, many persons took part, but if the reporter had looked up from his notes to see who was talking each time someone interjected a comment, he would have been far behind in his transcript. So my friend made a study of voices. I think if that man had ever heard a voice anywhere, he could instantly place that voice when he heard it again. He might not remember the man's face but he would remember his voice.

"This man had received a legal education and his experience in reporting hearings gave him a background of practical experience so it was an easy matter for him to pass the bar examination and enter the practice of law. During the years that he was my partner, when we were in court together, he made it a point not to look at the witness on the stand; he kept his eyes on a piece of paper, sometimes taking down what the witness was saying in shorthand, sometimes simply doodling, but always listening to the voice of the witness.

"At some stage in the examination my partner would nudge me with his elbow.

"Invariably that meant that the witness was either lying at that point in his testimony, or was trying to cover up something.

"My untrained ears were never able to detect these

subtle changes of voice and tempo, but my partner could spot them with startling accuracy."

SPOKEN WORDS HAVE PERSONALITY

Gardner is talking about a skill that is not acquired through reading improvement courses. In print, a word is a word—black against white. When spoken, a word comes to life. It has everything from a facial expression to a stage setting all of its own.

The simple word "oh" says little as you see it printed here. But in spoken form, "oh" can acquire scores of meanings. According to the way in which it is spoken, "oh" can mean: "You surprised me"; or "I made a mistake"; or "You're a pain in the neck"; or "You make me so happy"; or "I'm bored"; or "I'm fascinated"; or "I understand"; or "I don't understand."

Definitions of this simple word can be altered by simple changes in voice or gestures, each of which give a new twist to the two letters.

As you may see from this simple example, the nonverbal messages that we receive as listeners reinforce, modify or even contradict the words that a talker speaks. Sometimes the nonverbal part of the communication received by the listener is far more important than the verbal part. This is certainly true when the word "oh" is employed.

The wordless language that accompanies what we hear becomes vastly complicated when we try to pin it down. All of our senses become involved, and possibly extra-sensory perception plays a role.

Touch plays a part in nonverbal communication. What happens when you receive a hearty "how-do-you-do" but at the same time your hand receives a handshake that feels like a cold, wet towel?

Physical distance between speaker and listener has something to say for itself. There's the man who comes too close and the one who won't come close enough. Both of them modify what they have to say by the distance they keep.

The words we hear may be given additional meaning by the way a talker holds his cigarettes, or toys with his glasses at certain moments, or adjusts his belt, or bites at a fingernail, or squints his eyes, or adjusts his necktie.

A slip of the tongue or a fumble for words may say more than the smoothest portions of language that we hear. A change in tone of voice can betray a lump in the throat that has more meaning than the forthcoming words.

The way a talker wears his clothes, washes his face, combs his hair, keeps his desk, or arranges his furniture can all broadcast certain nonverbal messages that have their effect upon what the person speaks in words.

Because of such manifestations when he speaks, the talker is in a position where he is bound to give more of himself than is usually the case with the writer. Every tone he utters, every twitch of his muscles, every flick of his eye is likely to betray what he has on his mind.

LISTENING TAKES ENERGY

The listener, then, has far more to assimilate and to work with than the reader. But to do a good job of listening, the listener must also give more of himself. If he is to receive fully everything a talker has to offer, the efficient listener must stay alert on several fronts. He works with his ears, his eyes, his whole being.

In our listening classes at the University of Minnesota we continually stress the fact that good listening takes an enormous amount of energy. It is not a passive activity in which we can lie back, relax and just allow the words to pour into our ears. Good listening draws upon all of our senses as receptors, and it requires large amounts of mental energy to sift and store everything that is available through the senses.

This chapter should have made you aware of two important factors that must be considered for good listening: (1) the differences between oral and written language, and (2) the importance of nonverbal communication. Anything you can do to increase your awareness of these two factors will help you as a listener. For example:

+ Try analyzing how people compose their sentences when talking off the cuff. If possible, make a recording of some people engaging in everyday conversation. Play back the recording several times and note how they talk.

+ After listening to someone speak on the radio or television, try to obtain a verbatim text of the speech. Read it carefully, trying to determine whether the speech was extemporaneous or was written down first and then read aloud.

+ While watching television or a movie, shut off the sound by turning down the volume or plugging your ears for a minute. How much information can you get from just what you see?

+ Reverse this procedure so that you listen but do not look. How much do you feel you lose by cutting off your visual aids to listening?

+ In a public place you can often see people talking with one another, but can't hear them. In such cases watch carefully, trying to see what their facial expressions and gestures convey to you.

✦ Many times we can hear people talk but are not close enough to understand every word. In such a case, see what information you can glean just from the variations of tone, timbre, volume and rate of speed at which the words are spoken.

Chapter 6

The Architecture of What We Hear

One time a church was torn down in Europe and shipped stone by stone to America, where it was re-assembled in its original form.

The moving of the church, it occurs to me, is analogous to what happens when a person speaks and is understood by a listener.

The talker has a thought, which we might compare with the church. To transmit his thought, he takes it apart by putting it into words, which we might compare with the stones. The words are then sent through the air to the listener, who must reassemble them into the original thought if they're to be thoroughly understood.

But, thinking back to the real church, what if the stones had been received in America without any plan revealing their original structure? It's unlikely that the rebuilt church would look exactly as it did in Europe.

The same kind of difficulty is encountered by a person who does not listen properly. He lacks a plan for rebuilding what he hears. Words arrive from the talker one at a time. The listener pulls them together into facts, but seldom does he reformulate the ideas which would give sense and system to the facts being caught. As a result the talker's original thought is not accurately reproduced in the listener's mind.

REBUILDING IDEAS

In our studies of listeners we have noticed that some people are able to listen for whole ideas rather than bits and pieces of what is said. This ability is very often found in people who have studied public speaking. After learning how speeches are planned and constructed, they seem to have a better sense of how other people organize what they have to say.

In listening-training courses we have also found that listening ability improves if people can be given an outline of a talk before it is made. Often the outline becomes an important guide that helps to reconstruct the central ideas of the talk.

Obviously everyone who speaks to us doesn't first present us with a plan of what is to be said; however, there are general patterns in which people talk. If we know the patterns it is more likely that we can do a good job at reconstructing what we hear.

The most basic and important pattern for a listener to keep in mind is the one that reveals how an idea is structured. As stated briefly above, a talker ordinarily wishes to communicate an idea to the listener. Sometimes the talker may spend an hour building up an idea that, in its barest form, might be expressed in a simple sentence. His building blocks are words, but, no matter how you look at the communication process, the finished product must be rebuilt by the listener. He must pile the words into facts. The facts then become the pillars on which rests each idea that is communicated.

When this basic pattern is understood by people, they are likely to do a better job of listening. They listen for central ideas rather than for isolated words, sentences or facts.

But still the listener's building job can be made easy or difficult by the way the talker organizes the words he sends out. The aim of a trained public speaker is to make it easy for the listener to reconstruct his spoken thoughts. For this reason a public speaker such as a minister, a politician or a news commentator may spend hours preparing what he has to say. If you as a listener know the procedure he follows, it will help you assemble his spoken words into the ideas that are being communicated. So let's look carefully at how the trained public speaker organizes his material.

There are two main kinds of speeches: (1) an informative talk presenting an idea that the speaker simply wants to inform his listeners about, or (2) a persuasive speech presenting an idea that the speaker wants his listeners to accept, believe or act upon. The organization of a talk varies slightly according to which kind of speech is being presented.

With either kind, the speaker is likely to give a talk organized in four parts. Public speakers have been doing this for some 2,000 years, since the pattern was set by the great teachers and orators of Greece and Rome. Today the four parts are called, in their order of presentation in a speech: introduction, thesis, body and conclusion.

As the trained speaker builds his introduction he will probably say something to catch your attention and to put you on common ground with him. And frequently,

67

if he is going to use unusual words or terms in his speech, he will define them at this point. Here are a few ways that a speaker might introduce his talk.

+ By telling a humorous anecdote.

+ By stating something shocking to jolt listeners to attention.

+ By impersonating someone or dramatizing something in order to catch the audience's interest and good feelings.

+ By quoting a prominent authority or reading a passage from literature, an editorial, or another person's speech, as an entree to what he has to say.

The introduction to a talk is usually short. In a five-minute speech it ordinarily lasts only a half minute or so— a minute and a half at the most. In a ten- to fifteen-minute speech the introduction averages between two and three minutes. But even in longer speeches the average introduction seldom exceeds two or three minutes.

Many people seem to think that the introduction is a time to "plunge in," to try to get every word. Actually this is not the time to jump in so eagerly. The introduction is only for the purpose its name implies: to introduce the person talking by allowing you to observe how he handles himself and how he uses words.

GET THE THESIS

As the speaker finishes his introduction, the so-called amenities are brought to a close and he moves to the statement of his thesis. If there is any one time during his entire talk when you should focus intently upon what he says, it is now.

The speech thesis is important to comprehend because it usually tells you why the speaker has chosen to stand up before you and say what he is to say. It may even state the central idea of the whole speech, or at least give a valuable clue to that idea.

The thesis element of the speech is certain to be the shortest of the four parts. Sometimes it's only a carefully worded sentence. Usually the speaker feels that it's important enough for him to have memorized it word for word. Occasionally he will repeat it, intensifying his emphasis upon it.

In the thesis of an informative speech, the speaker usually opens himself up and gets directly at the core of what he has on his mind. For example, he might say: "I want to tell you why the government has operated efficiently since more than half of the Hoover Commission's recommendations have been put into effect."

In the thesis the speaker may go one step further. He may briefly state how he will give you the information that is to follow. For example, he might add to the above statement of the thesis: "The Commission's recommendations have been put into effect in three different ways. Let's consider each of them in detail."

Here, then, you have in the thesis the key to the structure of the whole speech. As a listener you can't afford to miss it or to misunderstand it.

In the persuasive type of speech, the thesis usually takes a different form. The speaker isn't always so willing to tell you exactly what his purpose is. His purpose may be to change your mind on some matter, but he prefers first to give you all the reasons why you should change your mind before asking that you do so. For example, the thesis of a persuasive speech might be stated like this: "Before we make any changes in our government's organization, as citizens we may well ask ourselves three important questions. Let's consider those questions right now and come up with answers based on the facts at hand."

The speaker doesn't say which side of the fence he is on, for or against changing the government's organization, but you can bet that he has made a choice. So far he has only told you his procedure, that he is going to pose three questions for your consideration. The answers, he hopes, will lead you around to his way of thinking on the subject.

Again, however, a foundation has been laid, and you, as a listener, should have been tuned in while the job was being done—or the listening from that point on may not be so easy.

THE EVIDENCE COMES IN

When the thesis is stated completely, the speaker moves into the body of his speech, the longest part of the talk. It will use up two-thirds or more of a short speech, and a greater proportion of a long speech.

The body of the speech supports the thesis by building a small number of main points capable of fully establishing that thesis. Each main point becomes a pillar upon which the central proposition of the speaker rests. There are several kinds of material that a speaker can use for point support. For instance, he may report statistics. Or he may illustrate the points he makes by drawing analogies, by using similes and metaphors, or by telling stories (anecdotes, fables, parables). At other spots in the speech body, the speaker may use testimony to support his thesis; he will quote an authority on his subject, for example. And of course, there are many other ways that he may verbally build up the speech's body.

The body of an informative talk ordinarily takes a different approach from that of a persuasive talk.

In the informative speech the approach is likely to be "deductive." In other words, the speaker will start each point that he has to make with a generalization which is then followed with the material that supports it. This is clear-cut procedure, and readily understood by most listeners.

The situation is turned around in the persuasive speech. An "inductive" approach is taken. In this case the generalization of each point is made *after* its supporting material has been stated. As you may see, through the inductive approach, the speaker has a better chance of leading the listener—often without his conscious knowledge—to the point where the speaker wants him.

What do you do as a listener during the third part of a speech? Your main goal, of course, is to comprehend what the speaker has to say. But also here is the place where you should appraise the speaker. You should question the support that he makes of his thesis. How valid is it? How recent is his evidence? Is he reporting all the evidence? If not, what is he leaving out, and why? In other words, the body of the speech is the part of which you should be most critical.

AND IN CONCLUSION...

Finally comes part four, the speech conclusion. In the informative speech the conclusion is usually a summary of what has been said plus some statements pointing out how the speech is important to those who are listening. Sometimes the speaker may also make a mild appeal to his listeners—asking them to put to work what they have learned from the talk.

The conclusion of a persuasive speech similarly starts with a summary, but still the speaker's complete purpose may not be clear. However, he then moves quickly into a final appeal revealing exactly how he feels about the subject of his speech. And, of course, how he feels is the way he would like to have his listeners feel. With everything in the open, the speaker then feels free to make as strong an appeal as possible; to do so he often drops logic and becomes emotional in his attempt to bring the audience around to his way of thinking.

During the conclusion the listener's main goal is again that of comprehension. But, more than ever, critical listening is needed. When the speaker makes his appeal, especially during the persuasive talk, his calm reasonableness may end. From the listener's standpoint it's a time when he should definitely question what he hears. Above all, however, he should reserve judgment so that he may— possibly after a cooling-off period—make up his own mind about what he has heard.

VERBAL WANDERLUST

So far, this discussion of speech structure is limited to the well-organized talk. However, the chances are that most of the speeches you hear won't be well organized. Comparatively few people are trained public speakers, and on occasions even the trained ones may give unorganized talks.

Much of what we hear is spoken "off the cuff." The words that are voiced are not systematically organized to support the ideas being presented. Indeed, many of the spoken words may have nothing to do with the central ideas that an unorganized talker attempts to communicate.

However, the fact that a talk is unorganized doesn't necessarily mean that it isn't worth listening to. In the welter of words there may be valuable ideas. But what can a listener do to catch these ideas?

If a speech has no logical structure, or if it is impossible for you to find one, the search for any kind of a pattern in the talk should end immediately. Such a search is usually fruitless, and engaging in it prevents you from hearing anything of value that might be said.

As you drop the search for structure, there are two things to listen for in the talk: (1) facts and (2) principles.*

If you spend your listening time trying to identify and group any facts or principles that emerge from the talk, your time will be used to best advantage.

In searching for facts, listen for the description of acts and deeds that really happened, or any statements that you can decide are strictly true.

In seeking out principles, listen for the speaker to describe the "essence" of things. He talks about "law, doctrine, rule, broad truth, or generalization." In other words, a principle is something that controls or gives system to a large number of facts.

Separating the two in a speech may not always be easy. But the effort will insure that your time is well spent during an unorganized talk. The facts you hear, when tallied up, may support the principles that you glean from the speech. If this is true, and you can see the relationship, you will be on the way to understanding the central ideas that the speaker is trying to communicate.

* In Chapter 10 see the note-taking system concerned with "fact versus principle" listening.

Of course most of our listening time is not used in hearing speeches. Most of it is employed in listening to conversation. On first consideration, conversation may seem like the most unorganized kind of talk we could possibly hear. But is it? Let's reproduce a typical conversation and then look for any pattern that may be there.

A man meets you on the street.

"How are you?" he says. "I was just thinking about you this morning. I was hoping to run into you."

You give your answers and the person continues talking.

"Say, what's this that I hear about you getting married? Do you really know what this means to a fellow like yourself? I bet you haven't thought about what it will cost you."

You answer again, and the conversation moves along.

"Well, it won't be the same for us boys. Your friends at the poolroom are sure going to miss you. Of course, it will make a big difference to your parents; they've been hoping that you would get married and raise a family."

You agree, and here we go again.

"Speaking of your family, your father is pretty excited about the marriage, I understand. He's a great guy. And your sister is happy for you too, but your brother Joe seems a little jealous."

This part of the conversation can go on for some time, discussing the different people involved, but, as you can see, the subject is about to change.

Doesn't this sound like a typical unit of conversation? Let's look at it for a pattern. Conversation, like a speech that is well organized, can usually be broken into four parts.

Part I: Verification of the status quo.

In this opening part of the conversation the talker speaks of things that exist right now. In the above conversation he asks how you are and then says he was thinking about you and hoping to see you.

Part II: Verification of problems that are ahead.

This part of the conversation is like the thesis of a speech. The talker suggests a purpose for saying what is about to come. He asks if you understand the problems of marriage.

Part III: Verification of who will be affected.

The problem is usually of interest only if it will affect people, so immediately the conversation turns to the human effect of Part II. Friends and family will be affected by your marriage.

Part IV: Discussion of personalities until the subject changes.

This part of the conversation may deviate from the problem but it has been prompted by Part III. The participants in this part dig deeper into the human element involved until the topic is worn out. Everyone is happy about your marriage except brother.

In general, these are the four parts to a unit of conversation. If the conversation lasts a long time, the pattern repeats over and over as you move from subject to subject.

How can a listener use this pattern to improve his listening? The answer is: Don't try—at least don't try too hard.

Comprehension of facts and ideas is the primary goal for listening to conversation. But—and maybe it's fortunate—most conversations are not overloaded with ideas. Conversation is more likely to be a form of talk that you can look upon as entertainment.

However, it may be fun to watch the above pattern at work in conversation. Certainly understanding the course that a conversation takes will not harm what you can get from it through listening, and it may improve your ability to understand the other participants.

Sometimes, in a conversation, one individual falls into the role of a leader, guiding the other members through one topic of conversation to another. If this role falls upon you, knowledge of how conversation is normally constructed may help you do a better job.

Chapter 7

The Ears Can Concentrate

One time at the University of Minnesota, I asked a large group of students to write down all of the things that they were certain had impaired their ability to listen at some time or another. From the students' reports came a list of 107 different factors that were known to have adversely influenced the listening process.

Grief, joy, anger, self-consciousness, fear, worry and laziness were all listed. One student had been affected by stormy weather. Chewing gum had disturbed another person. Certain color combinations on the wall had bothered one person. Economic strain had prevented more than one student from doing his best when he listened. Being seated among enemies had been detrimental to listening in another case. And a toothache had ruined listening in several instances. All of these factors reported by the students affected their ability to concentrate.

CONCENTRATION IS DIFFICULT

In general, people feel that concentration while listening is a greater problem than concentration during any other form of personal communication. Actually, listening concentration is more difficult, and there's a reason for it. When we listen, concentration must be achieved despite a factor that is peculiar to aural communication, one that few people are aware of. Basically, the problem is caused by the fact that we think much faster than we talk.

The average rate of speech for most Americans is around 125 words per minute. This rate is slow going for the human brain, which is made up of more than 13 billion cells and operates in such a complicated but efficient manner that it makes the great, modern digital computers seem simple-minded. People who study the brain are not in complete agreement as to how it functions when we think, but most psychologists believe that the basic medium of thought is language. Certainly words play a large part in our thinking processes. And the words race through our heads at speeds much higher than 125 words per minute.

In the field of reading there are examples of how fast the brain can handle words. It is common to find people who read and understand 1,200 words per minute, and even much more. A University of Florida student was reported to have scanned for facts at the rate of some 10,000 words per minute and to have scored over 80 per cent on factual tests covering the material.

Experiments in the field of speech show that people can do a good job of listening to words spoken much faster than the average of 125 per minute. It has been found that people can comprehend speech at more than 300 words per minute without significant loss from what can be comprehended and retained at much slower speeds. Theoretically, many more spoken words per minute could be understood, but there's a limit to the speed at which words can be formed orally without a mechanical distortion resulting in unintelligibility.

The brain deals with words at a lightning pace, but when we listen, we ask this brain to receive words at an extremely slow pace. It might seem logical to slow down our thinking when we listen to coincide with the 125-word-per-minute speech rate. But slowing down thought processes is a difficult thing to do—almost painful. Therefore, when we listen, we continue thinking at high speed while the spoken words arrive at low speed. In the act of listening the differential between thinking and speaking rates means that our brains work with hundreds of words in addition to those we hear, assembling thoughts other than those spoken to us. To put it another way, we can listen and still have spare time for thinking.

What do you do with your spare thinking time as you listen? The answer to this question holds the key to concentration in listening.

ON-AND-OFF LISTENING

In our studies of listeners at the University of Minnesota we find that most people do not wisely use their spare thinking time as they listen. Let's illustrate how this happens by describing an experience that most people find familiar. Assume that you're listening to a friend at lunch in a restaurant. He tells you about a problem he met on his job. Your listening may work something like this:

He starts talking and you perk up your ears. Sounds interesting, so you decide to listen to everything he says. You have no trouble understanding him. Indeed, it is extremely easy.

A waiter walks by with a frozen éclair topped with whipped cream. "Looks good," you think momentarily, quickly returning your thoughts to what your friend is saying.

Subconsciously you know that you can think of other things as you listen, that you have time for your mind to dart in and out from the line of thought being spoken to you. The extraneous thought about the éclair doesn't prevent you from following your friend's line of thought.

"Frozen éclairs with whipped cream are extremely fattening," you suddenly think. "I won't order one, much as I would like. . . ."

This thought took you away from your friend's talk a little longer, but the time out was still no bother. At the rate he talks you can sandwich many thoughts between his words, phrases and sentences and still comprehend all that he says. So you continue jumping back and forth mentally, listening, tuning out your friend, tuning in some of your own thoughts and then tuning back to him.

But these private excursions from his line of thought are dangerous. On one excursion you're bound to run into an especially enticing thought of your own.

"It's only three weeks before vacation," you remind yourself. "I sure will be glad to get away for a few weeks. Going south in February will do the whole. . . ."

Suddenly you wake up from your reverie remembering to tune back to your friend. "Whoops! What was that he just said?" You stayed away too long and missed the tag end of a sentence. "Oh, well, what difference does it make?"

But it does make a difference. Your friend is now a little harder to understand. You have missed something in his line of thinking, and subsequently it may not be as easy to reassemble the thoughts that he is putting into words for you.

The disintegration of your listening has begun. In the face of the tougher listening situation, some of your private thoughts are now more enticing than ever. They're easier to live with than those your friend is trying to convey to you. Each mental jaunt into your own world of thought is likely to be longer than its predecessors. And you miss more and more of what your friend says.

Eventually you give up listening. It's too hard. You simply think your own thoughts, although you nod your head and grunt occasionally to act like a listener for the sake of courtesy to your friend. Of course, you frequently tune back to him for split seconds at a time. After all, he might be asking you a question. But this is not listening; now you're only monitoring the spoken word.

This example may sound as if the listener doesn't care about understanding what is said. It could be, but it also could be that the listener cares very much about what is said. The business of progressively tuning away from a talker until we lose his trend of thought is a bad habit that bothers most of us.

Behind this habit lies the fact that few of us have had the opportunity of learning how to use our spare thinking time when we listen. It's frequently used for very personal—often recreational—purposes, and therefore extraneous thoughts eat into the listening process to the point where communication operates at a far lower level than it should.

ON-THE-TRACK LISTENING

A major task in helping people to improve listening is that of teaching them to use their spare thinking time efficiently as they listen. To find what efficient use of this time consists of, I made an extensive study of people's listening habits, especially trying to discover what happens when people listen well. During this study it became obvious that good listeners regularly engage in four mental activities, all of them closely geared to the oral discourse and taking place concurrently with that oral discourse. These four mental activities are neatly coordinated when listening works at its best. They tend to direct a maximum amount of thought to the message being received, leaving a minimum amount of time for mental excursions leading away from the talker's thought.

Here are the four mental processes in a listener's mind when he is doing a good job of receiving and fully understanding the spoken word.

1. The listener thinks ahead of the talker, trying to guess what the oral discourse is leading to, what conclusions will be drawn from the words spoken at the moment.
2. The listener weighs the verbal evidence used by the talker to support the points that he makes.
3. Periodically the listener reviews the portion of the talk completed thus far.
4. Throughout the talk, the listener "listens between the lines" in search of meaning that is not necessarily put into spoken words.

The speed at which we think compared to that at which people talk allows plenty of time to accomplish all four of these mental tasks when we listen.

TORTOISE TALKERS—HARE LISTENERS

Talkers and listeners are like the tortoise and the hare in the well-known fable. Poor listeners eventually end up in the predicament of the hare who raced the tortoise. He stepped to the side of the path and went to sleep; the tortoise passed him up and won the race. When the hare woke up it was too late to catch up. Poor listeners go off on mental tangents, and when they return, the tortoise-paced talker is out of reach in the thoughts he's expressing.

But for purposes of analogy let's assume that the tortoise is a voice slowly proceeding down a spoken line of thought, and the hare is an efficient listener getting the most out of what is said.

The hare would start with the tortoise, but soon he would race ahead, trying to figure out what the tortoise would be saying when he arrived at various points along the path.

Then the hare would return to the tortoise and circle him. Meanwhile he would carefully weigh the tortoise's words.

Next the hare would race back along the path behind the tortoise and think of what had already been said.

And his fourth step would be to return to the plodder, hop a little to the side of the path and take a good over-all look at the tortoise. At this point the hare would try to determine if there was anything about his slow-paced friend, other than what he says, that could reveal something about the way he thinks.

The hare's gyrations would then start all over again, repeating themselves until the tortoise had reached the end of his path.

The hare's procedure is analogous to what the best listeners do mentally. They move back and forth along the talker's path, viewing it from four different angles. They capitalize their inherent advantage of thought speed, making it an asset rather than a detriment to listening. Their actions minimize the risk of becoming lost in the forest of distractions surrounding the talker's path. These listeners do much more than absorb the literal content of the words they hear. What they learn by listening has several dimensions. And they are the listeners least troubled by "inability to concentrate."

Right now, the idea of traveling four thought-process channels while listening to one voice may seem impossible. Indeed, it does require training. But with practice the four-way mental exercise can be turned into a habit which operates automatically when you listen. Let's look more closely at these channels to see what you do when you use them as a listener.

1. Thinking ahead

When a person talks to you, even informally, he usually tries to make a point. Sometimes in the course of his talk he makes several points, all of which add up to support one major proposition or idea. This is also what happens in the formal speech, as we found in Chapter 5. The speaker has a central idea that he wants to put across. He usually presents it in a statement of thesis early in his speech and then supports it with a number of points, which he makes one at a time.

The good listener tries to guess what these points are before they are made. As he listens he takes a moment here and there to ask: "What is this person trying to get at? What is it he wants me to believe or understand?" If there's no logical conclusion the listener guesses one.

Here is a guessing game that pays off whether the guesses are right or wrong. If the listener guesses correctly what a talker's point will be, his understanding and retention of the point will be strengthened when it is finally made. In effect he hears the point twice.

What happens if he guesses wrong? In this case the listener instinctively starts comparing the point he guessed with the actual one made. In so doing he engages in a highly profitable learning process, that of learning by comparison and contrast, a process advocated by educators from the time of Aristotle.

2. Weighing what you hear

The points that a person makes when he talks to you are usually constructed of at least three kinds of raw material. This material is his evidence. If you, as a listener, identify and evaluate these three kinds of raw material as they are spoken, you will increase the effectiveness of your listening.

The first kind of raw material used by a person talking is *straight exposition*. Exposition means explanation. The person talking explains how something works, why something happened, what something means, who someone is, and so on. With this kind of raw material, he defines and classifies what he has to say.

There are good explanations and poor ones. An effective listener uses part of his thinking time to decide whether or not the expository material he hears is valid. And, of course, he does his best to understand the explanations that he hears. Both purposes are assisted by answering the following questions while listening: "What has all this to do with me? Are things exactly as he says they are? Is he leaving anything out of his explanation? How can I use the information he is giving to me? And is this explanation clear enough to me so that I can report it accurately to someone else?"

The second kind of raw material used by people talking is *emotional appeal or harangue*. This kind of talk is not aimed at reasoning processes; it strikes at the listener's fears, hates, loves or any of his basic instinctive drives. The talker usually tries to get the listener to do or believe something for such causes as love of country or family, future security, revenging a wrong, or preserving the status quo. Sometimes such appeal turns into a harangue, with names called and abusive language used.

What does an effective listener do? When he identifies the above material, the listener tries to remain objective, to avoid emotional entanglements. Again there are helpful questions that the listener can ask of himself: "Why is this person so aroused? Does he have any solid evidence mixed with his emotional appeal? Are the motives behind his emotionalism justifiable?" And again if the listener listens with the idea of accurately reporting what he hears to someone else, it will help his listening comprehension and also his ability to see through the purely emotional content of the talker's words.

The third kind of raw material is *illustrative*. In this instance, a person talking usually states his point, illustrates the point, and then makes a generalized statement about the illustration to show that it is a typical case. For illustrations, people usually tell stories, each of which serves as a case history that is supposedly typical of the majority of cases. The person talking starts out by saying something like: "Let me tell you what happened on Main Street this morning." He weaves a story and concludes by saying something like: "Now, isn't that typical of what the bus drivers are doing to us passengers?"

But an oral illustration doesn't need to be a long, involved story. It can be a simple anecdote, fable, parable, figure of speech or analogy. The phrases "for example," "consider the case of," or "for instance" will often tip off the listener as to when the talker is about to illustrate a point.

Illustrative material appeals both to the listener's reason and his emotions. When it is used, the listener should be primarily concerned with determining the validity of the illustration. Is the story really typical of the majority of cases? Is a short anecdote sufficient evidence to make the point presented by the talker? Is the illustration out of date? Has time changed its applicability to the point being made?

Examples of such questioning that a listener can engage in might be as follows:

"The actions of a Michigan farmer toward the rural school in his area aren't necessarily representative of how the nation's farmers react to schools—or are they? What George Washington said and did about the Federal government may mean nothing today—or does it? The management policies of a successful Texas manufacturer should work in all manufacturing—or should they?"

This kind of questioning of illustrative material does two things. It helps the listener keep on the talker's path, and it evaluates the talker's material as he moves from point to point.*

3. Reviewing what you have heard

As the person talking moves from point to point, he usually allows time for you to move along with him. He will hesitate, to think of what to say next. He will say something transitional in nature, like: "Now let me talk about this matter of ..." As the talker takes time to move to his next point, the efficient listener takes the opportunity to review what has been said. He mentally runs over the points already made, stopping a split second with each one. Such a review prevents the listener from going off on mental excursions away from the talker's line of thought, and the review definitely improves both comprehension and retention of the material that is heard.

* For further discussion about "weighing what you hear" see Chapter 11, which covers critical listening.

4. Listening between the lines

What a person doesn't say may be even more important that what he does say. As he listens, the listener has time to search for hidden meanings in what is *not* said—to "listen between the lines." Does the talker skirt a point with great care? Are there failings or wrongs that the talker might admit but doesn't? Does his silence on a matter indicate it is a sore point with him?

Here also is a time for the listener to analyze in his mind the meaning of the talker's nonverbal communications (discussed in Chapter 4). What does the pounding of a fist on the table mean in relation to the words spoken? A sudden change in skin complexion may say more than the words heard at the same moment. The person starts talking faster and in a higher pitch of voice. What meaning do these changes add to the spoken word?

By mentally adding the meaning of what he hears to the meaning that he gets from what he doesn't hear, the listener can learn much about the proficiency, integrity and motives of the talker. Also a degree of comprehension can be attained that will never be reached when the listener hears only the literal content of the words that enter his ears.

CONCENTRATION IS THE RESULT

If a listener works at all four of these mental activities his ability to concentrate is certain to improve, for there will be little time to attend to mental tangents leading off into the world of distraction.

Chapter 8

Emotional Filters

When anyone asks me to describe the worst listener I ever encountered, an interesting experience with a freshman college student comes to mind. Not long after he started college, the student came to me for help. He was failing in many of his courses, and he had traced the difficulty to his inability to learn from lectures. In high school his grades were not bad, but at that point he had had few lectures. In college, however, listening to lectures was a daily experience.

"I go into a class with good intentions," he told me, "but as the professor continues to talk and talk, he gets on my nerves. Before long I can't even bear to listen to him."

This student visited my office a number of times. I tried to help him with his listening problem, but it was difficult to discover its basic cause. We approached the problem from a number of angles and finally hit upon what I think was the reason behind his failure at listening.

One day the boy began to tell about his life at home. He didn't conceal the fact that for years his mother had irritated him.

"She wouldn't leave me alone," he said. "From the time

89

I was very small she never ceased talking and complaining to me. It seemed that I could never say a word. She would start talking the moment I got up in the morning. Eventually I learned simply not to listen. I guess I would sort of reach up to my brain and turn her off."

From his experience the boy had come to dislike any kind of sustained discourse, and he would mentally tune it out. We decided that this "reaching up and turning off" was what happened in the classroom lectures. As a professor talked on and on, it became unbearable, and the student would reach up and turn off the lecture.

This problem was more than we could cope with in our listening courses. I recommended that he obtain psychiatric help, because there seemed to be psychological difficulties that needed attention. Meanwhile, however, his listening problem continued, and it made a failure out of his first year of college. Try as hard as he could, it was impossible for the student not to reach up and turn people off when they talked any length of time.

EMOTIONAL EARS

In different degrees and in many different ways, listening ability in all of us is affected by our emotions. Like the troubled college student we often "reach up and turn off" what we don't want to hear. Or, on the other hand, when someone says what we especially want to hear, we open our ears wide, accepting everything—truths, half-truths or fiction.

We might say, then, that our emotions act as filters to what we hear. At times they, in effect, cause deafness, and at other times they make listening altogether too easy.

When the emotions produce deafness, it can happen like this: If we hear something that opposes our most deeply rooted prejudices, notions, convictions, mores or complexes, our brains may become overstimulated, but not in a direction that leads to good listening. We mentally plan a rebuttal to what we hear. Or sometimes we formulate a question designed to embarrass the talker. Or perhaps we simply turn to thoughts that support our own feelings on the subject.

When emotions make listening too easy, it usually results from hearing something which supports our deeply rooted inner feelings. When we hear such support, our mental barriers are dropped and everything is welcomed. We ask no questions about what we hear; our critical faculties are put out of commission by our emotions. Thinking drops to a minimum because we are hearing thoughts we have harbored for years in support of our inner feelings. It's good to hear someone else think those thoughts, so we lazily enjoy the whole experience.

Of course these human reactions are not unique to listening. They operate, for instance, when we read or observe the world around us. But the reactions, as they apply to what we hear, create a problem that is unique to listening. It is simply this: When our emotions overstimulate our brain, it becomes more difficult to listen effectively; meanwhile important things may be spoken that will never be repeated for us.

What we are calling "emotional filters" have affected mankind from the beginning of time. When words have been spoken that support man's beliefs, he has usually listened and passed the words along down through the centuries. But when the words have not supported his beliefs, man has seldom listened and has not passed the words along to us.

Most of the legends that have come to us from distant times by word of mouth have been stories that supported the listeners' feelings about their countries, their races, their ideologies, or themselves.

"Your great, great grandfather," the father tells his son, "carved a thriving farm out of a rocky Vermont hillside. He got up every morning at 4 A.M. and worked until long after dark. The work that he did would have killed most men today. But the old man lived until he was ninety-three years old, and he worked up until the day he died."

The son listens and feels proud. The story tells him that he comes from ancestral stock which certainly must have transferred some of its greatness to him. He remembers the story, and years later passes it on to his children.

On the other hand there are stories bound to die before many generations have passed.

"Your grandfather on your father's side," whispers a mother to a son, "was a drunken thief. He was in jail more than he was out. His family starved during . . ."

If such a story were told, it would be unlikely to survive for long in a family. Too many family members would reach up and turn it off. Who wants to be the descendant of a drunken thief who would permit his family to starve?

The legend of George Washington and the cherry tree has come down through the years mostly by word of mouth. Children have listened and grown up to pass the story along to their children. Through the story each child can emotionally identify himself with the father of his country who in his childhood could not tell a lie. It's doubtful that a story presenting Washington in an unfavorable light could have survived as well.

THEY'RE ALWAYS SIFTING

Emotional filters are at work to affect nearly everything we hear.

Whenever we make a decision about something, there's a chance that our emotions will produce deafness when we hear something that could prove the decision wrong.

From studies of how people make their voting decisions in national elections, Columbia University's Bureau of Applied Social Research found that voters are affected by emotional deafness in listening to campaign oratory. Long before election day many people have decided how they will vote. These people tend to listen to speakers who support their decisions, but are not likely to listen to opposition speakers. For example, in the 1940 campaign for President, the Columbia researchers found that more Republicans than Democrats listened to Wendell Willkie, while more Democrats than Republicans listened to Franklin D. Roosevelt.

From our experience and education we build mental pictures of the way things "should be" in the world around us. When there's a chance of hearing something that might recast these images, emotional deafness is likely to occur.

Not long ago, the managers of a large East Coast industrial firm came to work on a Monday morning to find their plant surrounded by pickets. It was almost a complete surprise. Labor negotiations had been under way, but the top management had no idea that a strike was impending. It was the first strike in the firm's history. What had happened?

It developed that the firm's director of labor relations had personally warned a member of the top management that a strike was possible and had recommended action to prevent it. But the warning went unheard. The firm lost five days of valuable production before a settlement was reached.

Later, the management member who had been warned said his immediate reaction to the recommendations of the director of labor relations had been that "a strike couldn't happen here!" He had held that belief for years. There had never been a strike, so the executive felt that his picture of the firm's labor relations must be the right one. With that image firmly in his mind, he sat before the director of labor relations and only appeared to listen. What he was hearing didn't support his belief; therefore he "reached up and turned off" his listening. He never really learned the seriousness of the warning.

THE LISTENER'S FANTASY

Most of us at times engage in fantasy about the way we would like to be. In some degree we resemble James Thurber's character, Walter Mitty, who frequently lapsed from his real life into secret lives of fantasy. We tend to listen to almost anything that supports our secret feelings and aurally reject what doesn't support those feelings. A large segment of the nation's radio audience provides a clear-cut illustration of this thought.

For many years the radio "soap opera" has had strong listening appeal to a tremendous female audience that tunes in program after program religiously day after day. Many women do not want to miss an installment at any cost. In 1942 one avid soap-opera listener was convicted of murder and sentenced to die in the electric chair in the summer of that year. One of life's last worries for her was concerned with a soap opera. "I'm worried a little about *Abie's Irish Rose*," she said. "Every day I used to listen to it. But they discontinued the serial till September. I won't be here in September." The serial's producers heard about this worry, wrote a synopsis of the next season's story and sent it to the murderess.

Studies have been made of radio's daytime serials to find what so strongly attracts the woman listener. The studies show that, among other appeals to the female emotions, the programs lend strong emotional support to the secret lives of the typical woman in the nation's mass female audience.

In many of the soap operas the weak characters are usually men, while the strong are most often women. When firm leadership is needed, a woman usually fulfills the need. For example, in one serial an airplane is in trouble and the passengers are in danger of being blown up. There is "one chance in a hundred" of the plane landing without killing all the people aboard. The male passengers are powerless, but a woman named Stella Dallas steps forward and brings the plane safely to earth.

In the daytime dramas the rich and socially prominent characters almost always look with respect upon the attractiveness and efficiency of the middle-class female. In receiving such homage the middle-class woman is given social prestige and power that the soap-opera listener doesn't experience in real life but does in her fantasies. Ma Perkins, for example, is an elderly country housewife who owns a lumberyard and has a daughter. The daughter is married to a "brilliant" young congressman in Washington who often must look to Ma Perkins for advice. Through this situation, Ma Perkins wields great influence in the conduct of our national affairs.

Who are the troublemakers in soap operas? They are most frequently men. If there's trouble in a marriage, the male partner is likely to be at the root of the evil. If one marriage partner is unfaithful to the other, the chances are that the man is the villain. And when it comes to straightening out soap-opera troubles the women characters ordinarily must shoulder the burden alone.

Age is something that has little effect upon the lady characters of some soap operas. The daily radio installments continually prove that the middle-aged woman is still in the prime of life, that she need not miss a bit of what life offers to all women. Helen Trent is a good example. Her activities illustrate to listeners that there's plenty of opportunity for romance in middle age, and even in the years following that period.

Through such dramatic devices many female listeners hear what they want to hear from the soap operas; so they listen to episode after episode. The programs lend support to the daydreams, the secret lives, of the listeners. If Ma Perkins or Helen Trent—both ordinary womenfolk—can do what the housewife at the kitchen sink longs to do, her longings possibly have credence.

On the other hand, the man of the house is not likely to be caught tuning in soap operas, even if he's around a radio in the daytime. Such dramas do not present what he wants to hear. Exposure to the programs would soon cause emotional deafness. The man is more likely to listen to a nighttime detective drama, western horse opera, or anything with high adventure where men are strong and take care of the weaker sex as females should be cared for.

STOP, GO, REVERSE

So far in this chapter, the effect that emotional filters have on listening has been presented as though the problem were either black or white, as though emotions either cause deafness or, on the other hand, make it too easy to listen. This is true to a great degree, but actually the problem is still further complicated.

These emotional filters become very tricky at times. They may block a word or phrase trying to enter our ears. Or they may let certain words or phrases rush in with force, so that they are deeply impressed upon us. The filters also have a way of turning things around when we

96

hear them, changing meaning so that it's entirely different from what was spoken.

While we listen the emotions may, in effect, say to our brains, "You just heard some words that don't fit your way of thinking. Strike them out." A little later they may say, "Here are some words that do fit. Remember them well." Or the emotions may say, "What you're hearing now doesn't conform to your way of thinking. Change it around until it does conform. When it is altered, consider that that is what you really heard."

Let's see how all of this works.

Not long ago in New York City, Management Development Associates, a firm that specializes in industrial executive development, held a seminar with top-level managers from large firms. The seminar's instructor asked five of the executives to leave the room. Those remaining were requested to study a slide picture which was then projected onto a movie screen in front of them.

The viewers saw a scene inside a streetcar. People were seated along the sides of the car. In the center stood two men face to face, a Negro dressed in a business suit and a white man in working clothes. The white man held an opened razor down at his side in his left hand. It could easily be assumed that the men were arguing, but the streetcar passengers were paying almost no attention to what was happening.

The seminar's executives studied the picture and the projector was snapped off. An executive was asked to return from outside the room and listen to a description of the streetcar scene spoken by one of the men who had seen the slide. Another executive was then called into the room and asked to listen to the description as it was repeated by the first man entering the room. The same procedure was followed until all five men had returned, and the description had been relayed from one to another. This meant that the fifth man's knowledge of the streetcar scene had been transmitted to him verbally through four of his colleagues. He was asked to face the group with his back to the movie screen and tell what he understood the slide picture to contain. The projector was snapped on so the group could visually compare the slide with the description they were hearing.

In the last man's description, the streetcar scene had changed considerably. The Negro and white man were now "fighting." Other passengers were involved in the fight or extremely frightened. The most significant change that had taken place concerned the razor and the two men's clothing. According to the fifth man's description, the razor was in the Negro's hand. The white man had on a business suit and the Negro wore working clothes.

The change in the scene took place gradually as the description passed from one listener to the next. The first man did a fairly accurate job of describing what he saw, but each listener thereafter unconsciously made changes in the scene.

The man who had first said the razor was in the Negro's hand was later asked why he had put it there. He didn't know for sure, but answered, "Why, it's just natural to think that colored men carry razors, I guess." The man who had been responsible for mentally switching the work clothes and the business suit felt that he had done so because the majority of Negroes he had seen were workmen.

THE MENTAL PATTERNS

Most of us have listening problems similar to those encountered by the executives. As words are spoken to us they often carry ideas contrary to our firmly implanted mental patterns. Day after day these patterns build up from life's experiences. We learn to work with the patterns; they're part of our daily routine, for they're easy to follow. If something comes along to prove that the patterns are wrong, we unconsciously rebel. We don't want to hear about it. If we do hear, we may alter the incoming message so that it conforms to our mental patterns. Meanwhile, listening comprehension is at a low point indeed. We hear, but who can say that we hear correctly?

An amazing factor about most of our mental patterns is that each is often associated with a label, a word or two. We seem to loosely categorize our experiences by fixing them in our minds in patterns, and then sum up each pattern by affixing a label to it.

For example, suppose that everything that happened to you in your home town was pleasant. The words "home town" thereafter become a label which quickly brings pleasant thoughts into your mind. You don't have to spend time thinking through all the experiences back home; the two words are enough to think about, and to hear them will bring back a flood of good feeling. But even if, with passing years, the home town deteriorates and falls on hard times, no one can tell you that your "home town" isn't still the best place in the world. You hear the words and then stop listening. No one can tell you about the changes that have taken place.

Most of us use many such labels. We hear them and they trigger off a whole surge of emotions that we have learned to associate with the labels. When this happens emotions take over and logic is tossed out. At the same time we cease listening effectively.

The avid Democrat hears the word "Republican." In the Democrat's mind, perhaps the word is a label for a mental pattern formed from years of hard experience with politics. He has decided from his experience that Republicans are the tools of big business, that they're against the little fellow and for the rich. But the Democrat feels no need to analyze his concept or do any reasoning about it. He hears the word "Republican" and it releases all the emotions that would have been let loose if he had really thought about his past experiences. Meanwhile, the Democrat's listening ability drops to a minimum while his emotions take over.

The firm's accountant drops in to see the general manager and says, "I have just heard from the Bureau of Internal Revenue, and . . ." The general manager suddenly breathes harder and thinks: "That blasted bureau! Can't they leave me alone? Every year the government milks me of profits." Red in the face, he whirls and stares out the window. The label "Bureau of Internal Revenue" cuts loose emotions that stop the general manager's listening. In the meantime, the accountant is going on to say that there's a chance to save $3,000 this year if the firm will take the proper steps. But the fuming general manager doesn't hear.

"Mother tells me," says the wife to her husband, "that . . ." But the husband hears little beyond the word "mother." Spoken by his wife, "mother" means "mother-in-law." The words form a label for a character disliked intensely by the husband. The mother-in-law had spent a week with the couple the previous year, and the husband tells his friends that it took him a month to get back into his wife's good graces. "The old lady turned my wife against me," he says. Now when he hears "mother" emotion rolls through his body and he ceases to listen.

Everyone holds in his mind a list of labels, emotion-laden words and phrases, that are troublemakers in the listening process. When the labels are heard the listener finds it hard to follow the person talking. He becomes distraught by what he hears, begins to think up embarrassing questions or fierce rebuttals, and the efficiency of communication drops close to the zero point.

LOCATING WORD BARRIERS

In my mind it would be a great service to education if researchers would seek out and identify "the one hundred greatest word barriers to learning." The words might be classified according to grade levels in school. With such a list, teachers could help their students to become aware of how these words often cause us to be guided by emotion rather than reason.

Over the years, from my own college classes I have collected words that have definitely handicapped students' listening abilities. Here is a partial list of the words: hick, kike, landlord, Jew, evolution, automation, red-neck, woolhat, sissy, sharecropper, venereal disease, Red, Communist, dumb farmer, antivivisectionist, nigger, yokel, hick town, square, and of course, Democrat and Republican.

Emotion-laden words which stand in the way of effective listening are tricky things. Many of them work at subconscious level where they can be coped with only through deep psychological searching that may require a psychiatrist's help. Others, some of the most troublesome ones, are close to the surface. We can deal with many of them and eliminate their effects as blocks to listening. Here are three steps that may help you cope with labels that hinder listening.

1. You should make every effort to become aware of the words that most upset you emotionally. It is often a good idea in this word-identification process to make a written list of them.
2. Once identified, the words should be analyzed.

Why do they affect you as they do? Was the acquisition of the words accomplished on a logical basis? Has an effort ever been made to see all sides of the situations to which the words have been applied as labels? And, most important of all, have the situations behind the words changed so that the words are no longer applicable?

3. You can rationalize the impact that such words have upon you by discussing them freely with other people.

By taking these three steps we often find that words and phrases which have emotionally upset us really need not bother us at all. Once this discovery has been made we can be fairly sure that they will do less harm to our listening ability.

FIGHTING THE FILTERS

But we still haven't considered all of the aspects of coping with "emotional filters." While listening, we are bound to be troubled by the very human desire to hear only what we want to hear and to turn off anything we do not want to hear.

The remedy—and it's far from being easily administered—can be summed up in the simple admonition: "Hear the man out!"

Following are three pointers that may help:

1. *Withhold evaluation.* This is one of the most important principles of learning, especially learning through the ear. It requires self-control, sometimes more than many of us can muster, but with persistent practice it can often be turned into a valuable habit. While listening, the main object is to comprehend each point made by the talker.

Judgments and decisions should be reserved until after the talker has finished. At that time, and only then, review his main ideas and make your assessments of them.

2. *Hunt for negative evidence.* When listening, it is human to go on a militant search for evidence which proves us right in what we believe. Seldom do we make a search for evidence to prove us wrong. The latter type of effort is not easy, for behind its application must lie a generous spirit and real breadth of outlook. However, an important part of listening comprehension is found in the search for negative evidence in what we hear. If you make up your mind to seek out the ideas that might prove you wrong, as well as those that might prove you right, you are less in danger of missing what people have to say.

3. *Make a realistic self-analysis.* Do people frequently step on your mental toes, causing you to become emotionally upset while they are talking? Do you often feel that the ideas of other people are wrong? Do you often find, as you debate some point that a person has orally made, that your argument turns out to be almost exactly what the person has said? If your answers are "yes," the time has come for you to make every effort possible to build a habit of "hearing the man out."

Chapter 9

Six Bad Habits

When I was a young boy I spent considerable time each week preparing for church on Sunday. I would save up things to think about while the minister was talking. One week I would decide to think about a .22 rifle, how I could save money for buying one and how wonderful it would be to go hunting with a .22. Another week I might save up thoughts about what to do when I grew up, whether to be an explorer, a railroad engineer or a band leader.

During the service on Sunday I would dig out my hoarded topics and think about them. As I did this, however, I would always assume the proper facial expression to make it appear that I was listening to the minister. I placed my elbow on my knee, rested my chin in my hand, fixed two glassy eyes on the minister, and then proceeded to have all the mental adventures I had been saving up for the occasion. The plan worked very well. I have to confess that as a boy I heard very little of what the minister said to his congregation.

Today I spend much time lecturing to college students. Frequently, as I look into their faces during a lecture, I will see a student, his chin resting in his hand, two un-blinking, staring eyes fixed upon me. Occasionally, just for fun, I stop my lecture abruptly, call the student by name, and ask him: "What do you think of that?" The question has the same effect as throwing ice water in his face. He suddenly jerks to attention and tries to cover up his lack of listening with some hurried remarks: "Oh, yeah, sure, I guess that's a good, errr...."

I have just been illustrating one of six bad listening habits that our research at the University of Minnesota has found to be almost universal. Each of these habits serves as a rationalization for not listening, even when the person who has acquired the habit knows and admits that he should be listening. One or several of the habits may apply to your own aural practices.

1. Faking attention

This is what I did as a boy at church and what a number of my students do in the classroom today. In succumbing to this bad habit we assume that if we look like listeners we satisfy all the requirements that a talker will ever expect of us.

If you're guilty of faking attention while listening you deceive only yourself. As you may have gathered several times from this book, listening takes energy. The expenditure of this energy leaves the listener looking, not as though he were cast from concrete, but as a very-much-alive human being who is following the spoken word with interest. The timing of his reactions is good because it occurs in a natural way. And when a person talking is finished, the real listener doesn't suddenly awaken as though he had been prodded with a hot iron.

If you're in the habit of faking attention, in all prob-

ability you're being caught in the act frequently. Furthermore, what's the point? You're only cheating yourself out
of an opportunity to learn from what is being said.

2. "I-get-the-facts" listening

Perhaps this habit is created by American movies where
newspapermen or detectives won't accept a moment's rest
until they "get all the facts." For some reason many people
seem to take great pride in being able to say that above
all they like to "get the facts." Very often they apply the
same maxim to the art of listening. It seems logical enough
to do so. If a man gets all the facts he should certainly
understand what is said to him. Therefore many people,
when they need to listen intently, try to memorize every
single fact that is spoken. With plenty of practice at "getting the facts" the listener, you can safely assume, will develop a serious bad habit. Here's what happens:

Let's say your boss is talking about something made up
of facts that we'll label A to Z. The boss begins to talk.
You hear fact A and think: I've got to remember it! So you
begin a memory exercise repeating "Fact A, fact A, fact
A . . ." Meanwhile, the boss is telling you fact B. Now you
have two facts to memorize. You become so busy doing
it that you miss fact C completely. And so it goes up to
fact Z. You catch a few facts, garble several others and
completely miss the rest.

Memorizing facts is not the way to listen. When people
talk they usually want you to understand their ideas. The
facts are only useful for constructing the ideas. Grasping
ideas is the skill on which the good listener concentrates.
He bothers to remember facts only long enough to understand the ideas that are built from the facts. But then,

almost miraculously, his grasping an idea will help the good listener to remember the supporting facts more effectively than does the person who goes after facts alone.

3. Avoiding difficult listening

A veteran of World War II who was a student at the University of Minnesota came to me one day for help in listening improvement.

"I was here in school before the war," he said. "But at that time, one year was all I could stand. I barely made it through the year. Taking in lectures and passing tests on them nearly killed me. I came to despise the whole business and when June of the freshman year rolled around I left school swearing I'd never come back.

"Frankly, I thought I wasn't college material. I felt that lectures were the toughest things in the world to learn from and that I wasn't smart enough to handle them.

"Well, I was drafted into the Air Force and they gave me an IQ test. It was the first I'd ever taken and I got a score of 120. They told me this was a pretty high score. After that I began wondering why that first year had seemed so tough. I still figure the trouble was involved with lectures, so now that I'm back here as a student I want to do something to improve my listening."

As we became acquainted, I found that this young man in his early schooling had seldom been subjected to any oral discourse that would have been difficult for him to understand. He lacked experience in listening to things that required much mental exertion. Later he came to feel that if things were difficult to understand there was little use in trying. Therefore he often avoided difficult listening.

This is a bad habit that many of us have. If we don't understand the man on radio or television we turn him off rather than stick it out and invest more energy in attempting to understand his words. The terms "lecture" and "public address" frighten many of us, and we stay clear of such functions. The discourses so labeled may require mental effort that we are not used to making.

The danger of this bad habit is that it can result in a diminishing downward spiral of listening ability. When one encounters any difficulty in understanding what he hears, it becomes a rationalization which, in effect, says: "Too hard to listen to; pass it up." Gradually the person moves from the easy listening to the easier listening, down and down. But ultimately one is certain to meet the situation where concentrated effort at listening is a must. The freshman for the first time in his life must listen to a difficult subject expounded by a professor who doesn't talk with the easily understood phrases of a radio comedian. The doctor carefully explains to a mother what she must do to care for her child. The boss outlines a new system that he wants carried out. But the listening experience creates tension. The listener has trouble trying to understand the words that are spoken.

If you are afflicted with this listening habit, the only solution is to make a planned and periodic effort to listen to difficult material. Listen to discussions of subjects that require mental effort on your part to understand, as, for example, in radio commentaries or panel discussions, or in lectures.

4. Premature dismissal of a subject as uninteresting

This bad habit works much the same as the one above, with the exception that the word "uninteresting" becomes the rationalization for not listening. Somehow many of us equate the term "interesting" with "valuable." If something lacks interest for us it often becomes a good reason in our minds for not listening.

The fallacy is that uninteresting talks very often have something to say that is very much worth hearing. Mrs. Claire Henry of Glenmount, New York, will undoubtedly testify to this fact.

Not long ago she listened to her husband talk shop, as he often does, about his telephone company job. Later she saw a trenching machine scoop a 5-foot ditch across a nearby piece of property. Because she had listened well, she knew that the machine was approaching a vital telephone cable. Her prompt warning prevented the cutting of the cable, which carried 3,000 important telephone and telegraph circuits and two television channels. The telephone company rewarded her with a four-day visit to New York City for her whole family.

To stop listening prematurely because you think a subject is uninteresting is a bad habit that can be broken by a planned effort of listening to all kinds of subjects. A selfish approach is suggested here. Even the most boring person ordinarily has some ideas to offer. Be selfish and take for yourself whatever ideas he may contribute.

G. K. Chesterton once stated that there is no such thing as an uninteresting subject; there are only uninterested people.

5. Criticizing delivery and physical appearance

One morning in the offices of a New York advertising agency an account executive had an appointment with a young copywriter. The young man claimed to have an idea for an advertising campaign. As he entered the executive's office the writer wore a plaid shirt. He began to tell about his idea, but the account executive took on the air of an iced flounder. Soon the young man wished he had stayed away. He cut short his talk and retreated from the office, assuming that his idea was not good. But then, over a year later, he tried out the idea again, this time by a memorandum which he sent up through channels to the agency's management. The idea was accepted and it resulted in one of the most successful advertising campaigns ever produced by the agency.

Why was the account executive so cold to the idea the year before? His secretary understood why. After the writer had left the office she heard her boss muttering about plaid shirts worn in business offices.

The account executive had hardly heard a word spoken by the writer. In the executive's mind, people who wear the wrong clothes to work are not worth listening to.

Many people use the same basic reason to rationalize bad listening. When someone talks to them they mentally criticize either physical appearance or speech delivery, or both. Perhaps the talker has a speech defect, such as a bad lisp, or has a foreign accent. The defects become excuses for not listening. "A person who talks like that can't have much to say," assumes the person on the receiving end. Or the listener becomes too critical of clothing, cosmetics, shoeshines, hairdos, and so on, and he assumes, "Anyone who looks like that can't have much to say."

All of this is not to intimate that physical appearances and manners of speech have nothing to do with what you hear. They do. They may tell you a great deal about the talker, but they should never serve as alibis for not listening to what he says. The *content* of the message is always far more important than the form of its delivery.

6. Yielding easily to distractions

A colleague of mine spent the summer of 1950 as director of a caravan for the Citizens Committee for the Hoover Report. The caravan consisted of a 30-foot stage-setting on a trailer truck. My friend traveled with it to nearly 100 cities around the country presenting outdoor programs in local business sections, with speakers explaining the Hoover report. He remembers very well what a struggle it was to hold an audience's listening attention.

"We battled distracting noises all summer," he says. "Our speakers outshouted the noise of buses, trolley cars, trucks, airplanes, autos and distant thunder to hold people's attention. Several times the battle was lost. In Circleville, Ohio, one evening the speakers were addressing 2,500 people when suddenly there was a screech of brakes down the street. A minute later less than 150 people remained in front of the caravan. The rest ran to the scene of what they supposed to be an accident. Actually, a dog had narrowly escaped being hit by a car, but few of the people who had gone from the caravan returned to listen to the rest of the speech."

This story is cited here because it's an exaggerated case of what many people do in the face of distractions.

The noise coming through the window competes with the person talking; the listener says to himself, "Too hard to hear." So he sits back, turning his thoughts to pleasant subjects of his own. The draft through the door makes it so uncomfortable for the listener that he finds it hard to concentrate upon the person talking. He continues to shiver, forgetting all about listening.

If you're a good listener you will not tolerate such distractions—by shutting a window, closing a door, moving closer to the person talking, requesting a noisy seatmate to be quiet, turning the heat down, or asking the person talking to speak louder. If distractions are overwhelming, then it's up to you to notify the talker; perhaps he will move to another environment more favorable for listening. Anyhow, your notifying him of the problem will be doing him as well as yourself a favor.

But there are situations where it's impossible to lick distractions, and you cannot interrupt the speaker. Then it is up to you to mentally shut out the distractions and turn your full attention to the talker. In other words, all of the techniques of concentration discussed in Chapter 7 are required.

Chapter 10

Pencil-and-paper Listening

The yellow, legal-size pad is a fixture in American business. Stationers report that the pads are selling more and more widely. In three years, a large New York City stationer, Alpha Office Supply Company, Inc., saw the annual sale of pads increase from 100 to 1,000 gross. They are used in many situations. When a conference table is made ready for a meeting, yellow pads and pencils are placed before each chair. When an executive's telephone rings, he reaches for a pad before taking the call. When the boss invites his subordinates to the head office, they arrive armed with yellow pads.

Millions of the pads are used each year for taking notes about what people have to say. Here's how the note taking works in many instances:

The note taker is thoroughly determined to record what he hears. The speaker starts talking and the man with the yellow pad assumes the writing position. As the words strike his ears, he commences to write. From long experience he knows that note taking is a tense race pitting his penmanship agility against the talker's rate of speech. Soon the man who is talking is winning the race. Good handwriting is discarded in favor of something more speedy: a hasty, illegible scribble. But still it's impossible to keep up with the talk. So the note taker now resorts to a telegraphic writing style with incomplete sentences and abbreviated words. Any chance this system might have had to work is lost by the time it is put into use, for the note taker has met an insolvable problem. Because he is concentrating on note taking he has lost track of what the talker was saying. What he is hearing doesn't even make sense anymore. The telegraphic style deteriorates to doodling, which becomes the listener's main function with the note pad until the talk is finished.

But obviously this man doesn't know how to take notes. He has no system. Let's see what happens when a person employs a commonly used method for note taking, the "outline system." He learned it in school by outlining chapters in books. In this system he works with many symbols: Roman numerals, capital letters, Arabic numerals, small letters, Arabic numerals in parentheses and small letters in parantheses. The symbols are placed before topics, sentences, and paragraphs of notes which are carefully indented in varying degrees along the yellow pad's left margin.

For a picture of how this system works, let's sample the note taker's thoughts some two minutes after the speaker has commenced talking. The thoughts run like this:

"Now Roman numeral III . . . no, no, it's number five under Roman numeral II. Now he was saying that 'men seldom bite . . .' Wait, wait . . . indent, don't forget to indent. Oh, curse this eraser. Now what was that he was saying?"

This fellow, it is clear, has become too involved in his system to do very much listening. He is using what proves to be a good note-taking system for some purposes, but one which frequently falls apart in many listening situations.

IS NOTE TAKING NEEDED?

For most of us, the ability to take notes when we listen is a desirable skill. The spoken word is ephemeral. As listeners we often feel the need for a written record of what we hear because we don't trust our abilities to recall. But when many of us try to take notes while listening —and find our system unsuccessful—we question the advisability of such performance. What is the answer?

In college, the students who keep good notebooks ordinarily do better than those who do not keep such notebooks. But a chicken-or-the-egg type of question arises here. Does the good student make the good notebook, or is it the other way around? This question is not fully answered to everyone's satisfaction.

However, existing evidence points out that *trained* note takers are better listeners. In a study that he made at Michigan State University, Dr. Charles Irvin concluded that "students who take notes are more consistent both in comprehension and in retention than those who do not." But at the same time Dr. Irvin found plenty of evidence which concludes that, in general, students do not know how to take adequate notes from what they hear. The students themselves feel this inadequacy. Dr. Irvin learned that 80 per cent of the students involved in his study wanted more training in note taking than they were then receiving.

For the person who uses a note-taking system which enhances and doesn't detract from listening there are several inherent advantages.

+ The very act of note taking, when done properly, is almost certain to improve the listener's attentiveness to the spoken words. If he is following a talker for the purpose of making a written record, the listener is less likely to sidetrack his thinking.

+ The taking of notes increases the chances that the listener will review what he has heard after he has heard it. Such review, as pointed out in previous chapters, is important to good listening.

+ And, when reviewed afterward, notes may remedy weaknesses in the listener's ability to learn from the spoken word. By reflecting upon his notes the listener may discover ideas transmitted from the talker that might otherwise have passed uncomprehended.

TO MAKE NOTES VALUABLE

Before considering two note-taking systems that enhance and do not detract from listening, there are a few general admonitions that should be considered. They apply to both of the systems to be discussed.

1. Keep them clear

By many people notes are considered useful simply as jogs to the memory. Therefore, their notes are written in words or phrases that do not carry complete thoughts. Such notes may serve a purpose if used soon after they're taken, but they rapidly lose their value as time passes. When possible, it's best to make each note a complete sentence. Sentences are the vehicles for thoughts, and thoughts are what we want to record in notes.

2. Keep them brief

Though important for clarity's sake, the effort to make complete notes should not be carried too far. The minimum amount of note taking possible is important. The reason is simple: While you're writing, your effectiveness as a listener is diminished.

3. Review them later

The proper kind of note taking has value, but its real importance is found only after a review of the notes. Too many people take notes and never use them. It would be better not to take notes at all, because the time spent writing can be better used by listening. If you take notes, schedule a definite time for their review and follow through on your schedule.

There are two note-taking systems which work well in a large number of listening situations. Both systems, when used effectively, allow the maximum time for listening and demand a minimum of time for writing. They are designed to record what most people are trying to communicate when they talk: *ideas*.

THE PRÉCIS WRITER

The first system is called "précis writing." With this system, the listener writes notes only at widely spaced intervals of time. When the talker begins speaking, the note taker sits back and listens, perhaps for two or three minutes. He then writes a short paragraph or a one-sentence abstract summarizing what he has heard. This spaced listening, followed by writing, continues for the duration of the talk. When he's through, the listener has a series of brief abstracts covering what was said.

Here's an example of how précis writing works. The note taker hears the following:

"An important leader in the Communist world did a strange thing on New Year's Day. He had planned to relax at his home in Moscow with his family. His grandchildren were visiting him and he is known to be especially fond of them. But in the middle of the day the official suddenly left Moscow for Budapest. At the same time rulers from Czechoslovakia, Rumania and Bulgaria rushed to Budapest. The four men held an all-night meeting. The communiqué issued about the meeting was remarkably uninformative. The leaders returned to their homes and immediately held secret meetings with their subordinates. The communiqués were issued from each of the leaders' capitals stating that the New Year was beginning with things going well all over the Communist word. All of this fits into a pattern that we have seen before. The pattern is usually followed by trouble for the Communists."

The note taker might write:

"Sudden secret meetings of Communist leaders are usually signals of forthcoming trouble for these men."

As précis writing is practiced, the times to listen and the times to write become obvious.* There is ordinarily a clear-cut breaking point between the main ideas set forth by a person talking. The breaking points between ideas are usually marked by transitional words or phrases, such as, "Now, let us turn to . . . ," "My next point is . . . ," or "Another matter for consideration is . . ." This is the point

* The discussion of oral language structure in Chapter 6 is important to an understanding of précis writing.

at which the note taker should do his writing if at all possible.

A talker's main ideas are usually spoken in units that include a generalization supported with explanatory material or an illustration. The generalization, which might come at the beginning or end of the unit, states the idea. The example concerned with the Communist leaders is a case in point. It begins with an illustration, a story of what the leaders did on New Year's Day, and it ends with a generalization, found in the last two sentencs of the paragraph.

As such idea-carrying units of talk are spoken, the efficient précis writer listens carefully, paying special attention to the generalizations. As he listens, he summarizes what he hears. At the end of a spoken unit that contains an idea, the note taker quickly writes his short summary, in a sentence or two, and then resumes listening for the next unit of talk.

But suppose the speaker talks too fast for writing the précis? Then the only thing to do is to put down a word or phrase that will remind the note taker of the idea that he has mentally summarized. But, if this is done, the note taker must come back to his notes as soon as possible after he has finished listening, and expand them to the point where they will be understandable after the passage of time.

In listening to a well-prepared formal speech there are two items for which a précis should always be written: (1) the thesis, and (2) the conclusion.

The thesis of a speech, as you may remember, is the statement of the speaker's purpose, or procedure, or both. It comes early in the talk, usually right after a short introduction. But summarizing the thesis of a speech in writing, when it is stated, is *not* the thing to do. The thesis is something that should be mentally grasped as soon as possible, and then considered throughout the remainder of the speech. Putting it into notes early in the talk will help neither the speaker nor the listener to achieve his purpose. Actually, the thing to do is to keep the thesis firmly in mind until after the speaker has finished talking, and then immediately to record the best possible statement of it in a summarizing sentence.

In the concluding passage of his talk, the speaker ordinarily makes a final appeal to his audience. He reiterates the importance of his proposals to his listeners, and openly asks for the action he desires.

This appeal is definitely worth summarizing in written form. When the notes are reviewed, mental reflections upon the speaker's appeal may reveal much about his speech that would otherwise be lost.

FACT-PRINCIPLE NOTES

The second effective note-taking system is that of recording "fact versus principle."

A large percentage of what we hear can not be classified as "organized." Many people simply do not know how to organize their spoken thoughts. Others, in this age of meetings and conferences, seem to have no time to organize what they say.

Most efforts at taking notes during a disorganized talk end in disappointment. The note taker is preoccupied by the question, "What's important and what isn't important enough to write down?"

For a note-taking system to work with a completely disorganized talk it should, in effect, collect the pieces so that at a later time they can be put together with some semblance of order. The pieces that are most worthwhile collecting are facts and principles.*

To collect them the note taker divides his paper into two columns, one for facts, one for principles. His listening efforts are then partly directed toward trying to determine what is a fact and what is a principle in the spoken words he hears. This task is not an easy one, but the effort itself is worthwhile, and any facts and principles that can be collected become a basis for usable notes.

To see how this system works, let's suppose that you're a sales and advertising executive for a company. One morning on the elevator, the chairman of the board says, "Come into my office as soon as you hang your coat up." In a few minutes you arrive in his office with a note pad. For an hour the chairman talks, touching upon this and that, but mainly hitting upon the company's advertising program.

The table on the next page contains fact-versus-principle notes that you might take away from his office. The content of the table reveals that the chairman is bothered by the company's approach in advertising.

Does he know what he's talking about? For the answer you would carefully compare the facts column with the principle column. Do his facts support his principles? Some do and some don't. A few of the facts seem irrelevant to the principles he had in mind. Two or three facts are very pertinent to the principles, but they really don't prove very much.

This set of notes would be far more valuable than page after page of scribbling that would be equally as mixed up as the chairman's words. From the notes taken you could prepare an intelligent rebuttal or program to meet what the chairman had on his mind.

* An explanation of how to recognize facts and principles is found in Chapter 6 in the discussion of listening to disorganized speech.

FACTS	PRINCIPLES
1. Indiana salesmen claim never see ads in papers.	1. People like to listen to advertising better than read it.
2. Chicago office receives no phone calls from ads.	
3. Competitor claims good results from ads on local radio stations.	2. Any advertising must be followed up by customer calls.
4. Thinking of hiring new radio copychief.	3. Word-of-mouth advertising can't be beat.
5. Neighbor's company sends ad men out to meet customers.	
6. Reader surveys report trade journal ads poor.	
7. Doubts company salesmen make enough calls.	
8. Two of our copywriters never been out of state.	
9. Several competitors give speech training to salesmen.	
10. No one ever asked our customers what they think of salesmen.	

There are two things that the listener can do to increase the effectiveness of the fact-versus-principle system of note taking.

✦ To be of real value these notes, even more so than those of other systems, should be carefully studied soon after they are made. In effect, the note taker must organize the speaker's thoughts. This organizing is done by mentally checking facts against principles for their relationship or lack of it. When the associations have been established between facts and principles, the emphasis for study should then be placed on the principles. If they are understood, remembering the facts that go with the principles will be easy.

✦ Oftentimes careful attention to the principles will show that they all relate to one another and that they add up to a single concept. For instance, the principles in the sample notes above might be brought together into one concept. They seem to say that advertising through the spoken word is more effective than through the written word. Trying to find such concepts will improve the efficiency of the fact-versus-principle system.

DON'T FRIGHTEN THE TALKER

There's one more facet to note taking that is sometimes extremely important, as a journalist friend of mine discovered early in his career.

One day he went to interview the chief of an important government bureau in Washington, D.C. The young reporter arrived in his best suit of clothes and proceeded to ask questions of the government man. The interview went well and the bureau chief responded freely to the questions that were asked. At one point something was said that the reporter felt to be very important. Until then his notebook and pencil had been kept in his coat pocket. The reporter reached for the book, flipped it open and prepared to write. That action, for all intents and purposes, killed the interview. The bureau chief's eyes, from then on, were fixed on the notebook, and the reporter could obtain no more information worth writing down.

For many people the idea of talking and being recorded in notes is a fearsome one, especially when they are talking "off the cuff" in an intimate face-to-face situation. They don't care to say the wrong thing and have it "recorded for posterity."

For anyone who finds it necessary to take notes in face-to-face interviews there are certain things he should do to minimize this fear of speaking for the record.

When the note taker meets his interviewee, he should have his note pad and pencil in plain view to prevent the note taking from coming as a paralyzing surprise in the middle of the talk.

Even before the interviewee starts talking, the note taker should ask for some information which, he says, he wants to write down. He might simply ask for the person's name and job title, or how long he has been in his present position. When the interviewer finishes his writing he might show it to the interviewee, asking, "Is that absolutely correct?"

This procedure does two things: It gets the person accustomed to the note taking and it may instill confidence in the note taker's ability to record accurately.

The note taker, when he first begins to write in the actual interview, should carefully observe the effect produced on the talker. If it makes him nervous, the note taker may be able to alleviate the condition by interrupting to read his notes back to the interviewee, asking, "Did I get this straight?"

If the note-taking process still bothers the talker, there's only one solution: the note pad and pencil should be put aside. The interviewer then has to depend solely upon his ability to recall later what he hears. When the interview is complete the listener then might pick up his notepad and say, "You had some important ideas to give me. I didn't want to bother you by taking notes. Will you please review them with me so I can get them down correctly?"

Of course, if there's no time left for a concluding review, the note taker must depend upon his memory and write his notes as soon as possible after leaving the interview.

Chapter 11

Listening To High Pressure

At the University of Iowa not long ago, 323 students, most of whom were freshmen, listened to a series of tape-recorded speeches on controversial subjects. The students were cooperating with Lawrence W. Brewster, who was doing research preparatory to writing his doctoral thesis. Brewster wanted to find out how critical the students would be of the speeches. He deliberately wrote the recorded talks with arguments that were weak in supporting evidence. After listening to the recordings, each student was asked to write a short commentary on some of the material that was heard.

In his thesis Brewster concluded that the students' written commentaries were unlikely to be critical of the ideas presented in the speeches. Instead of commenting on the recorded talks, most of the students only summarized what they heard.

There were, of course, some students who wrote critical evaluations of the speeches. Brewster noted that these students were "able to make more correct judgments as to whether certain statements were actually made or implied in a speech, and whether those statements, if made, were supported by evidence."

He also pointed out, incidentally, that according to his research the female students were somewhat more easily influenced by the speeches than the males. At the same time, Brewster was careful to say that the voice on the recordings was that of a man.

CRITICAL LISTENERS NEEDED

Brewster's research is in an area that certainly calls for attention. Critical listening is needed because words that are intended to persuade us vibrate our eardrums continually. The words may be uttered by politicians, faddists, lobbyists, or supersalesmen whose mellifluous tones are carried electronically across the countryside. These people have learned, sometimes instinctively, what Brewster's research reveals scientifically: People in general are credulous by way of the ear.

The ability to be critical of the spoken word is part of the responsibility that goes with freedom of speech. We have recently witnessed the downfall of a nation in which the responsibility for being aurally critical was not upheld. In a speech before the National Council of Teachers of English not long ago, Joseph Mersand, chairman of the English department, Jamaica, New York, High School, said:

"It was thought in the early days of printing that a populace that could read the printed page could therefore develop into a more civilized and cultured group. The sad spectacle of the most literate nation in Europe falling sway to the deceptive spoken words of Hitler smashed once and for all the notion that a well-read people was therefore a discriminating or thoughtful one. The era of dictatorship and totalitarianism has indicated to the world that our future civilization will be saved or destroyed by those who listen."

Wendell Johnson, well-known speech therapist and semanticist of the University of Iowa, stated the same problem in a different way when he said:

"As speakers, men have become schooled in the arts of persuasion; and without the counter-art of listening a man can be persuaded—even by his own words—to eat foods that ruin the liver, to abstain from killing flies, to vote away his right to vote, and to murder his fellows in the name of righteousness. The art of listening holds for us the desperate hope of withstanding the spreading ravages of commercial, nationalistic and ideological persuasion."

These are pleas for critical listening, a faculty that most people do not use often enough. Many of us, in learning to read, were taught to be critical of the written word, to ponder over it, question it and to "read between the lines." The same has seldom been taught to listeners, yet it is safe to say that we are exposed to more oral than written persuasion when we live in a world of telephones, radios and television sets. Critical listening is needed as much as, if not more than, critical reading.

And the critical listening need is not only confined to the area of persuasion. It exists in the dangerous areas of communication called gossip, rumor and the "grapevine." All of these depend mostly upon the spoken word rather than the written word. The rumormonger, gossip carrier and grapevine link are not critical of what they hear. Such listeners readily accept stories about other people or events, slander, predictions and "exclusive information" for which there is little or no basis of fact. Once accepted, the misinformation is almost always passed along in a more distorted form. Critical listening in our everyday con-

128

tacts with people is one answer to this form of twisted communication.

WHY CRITICAL LISTENING IS DIFFICULT

In intimate, face-to-face situations between listeners and talkers, at least six important factors, not found between readers and writers, work against the ability to be critical. (The first factor also applies somewhat to public-speaking situations.)

1. There is a time element. When reading persuasive material, there is usually ample time to reread and reconsider before action need be taken. But when we listen to persuasive words, the time for decision is often short, because in front of us is the persuader, a human being enveloping us in an active, living experience, and he often wants an immediate answer. What we hear, through words that quickly come and go, may serve as our sole evidence for a decision. Furthermore, the human factor in the spoken word, as opposed to static ink-on-paper words, throws additional weight behind the persuasion. It's far easier to say "No!" to a printed page than to a living being.

(One of the most effective persuaders I know is a salesman for a major oil company in Illinois. He would no more think of making a sales pitch by letter than he would of sending it from his office roof by smoke signals. His persuasion is oral and face-to-face if at all possible. He drives across Illinois all day and into the night to talk with a customer rather than to write him a letter, or even telephone him. The salesman knows that his physical presence adds force to what he has to say, minimizing the sort of critical tendencies that a client might use upon a sales letter.)

129

2. People in general are more effective at oral persuasion than at written persuasion. Comparatively few people write for persuasive reasons, but almost everyone has a vast experience at oral persuasion. We practice the art daily from the first twenty-four hours after birth when we fill the night with screams to persuade someone to leave a warm bed for nursing purposes. In time great numbers of us become extremely effective at oral persuasion, and in this world where critical listening is an exception to the rule, we may discover that with our spoken words we easily mold opinions and produce actions in other people as we see fit, sometimes to the benefit of others, sometimes not.

3. When people write, they sense—perhaps egotistically—that their words will be observed by great numbers of people. So writers are likely to "tighten up," become cautious of what they say. But the same people, in intimate conversations, usually drop such caution. They may color their language with humor and pathos if it serves their purpose. Sometimes they'll edit facts to fit arguments. Exaggeration is frequently employed. But even if they tried, it's harder to be accurate in conversation than in writing. The spoken words must keep moving; there isn't always time to make them accurate.

4. When people listen in chance encounters, such as in everyday conversations, they are likely to feel that the talker has no motive, no purpose behind what he says, other than the simple desire to talk things over. But this is not necessarily true; the talker may very well have a motive. Yet the listener, as a result of his false assumption, drops his defenses, becoming even less critical than usual, and he accepts without question much of what he hears.

5. Most of us like to get the "inside dope," to feel that we have exclusive knowledge on a subject. The written word is frequently recorded for many people to read, but the intimate spoken word often seems to be for one person, the listener. As a result, listeners are inclined to accept without question what they hear from individuals, just to satisfy a craving for "inside dope." The same seems to be true when we overhear something. It makes us feel that we are tasting "forbidden fruit," that we have our finger on the "public pulse."

6. From childhood we are often motivated to do things in anticipation of receiving a reward for our actions. As listeners, we're influenced by this same motivation. Listening to persuasive arguments, we feel that if we say "Yes" the talker will reward us. The reward is sometimes only a smile or pat on the back, but we like this because it satisfies our desire to be accepted by people. In hopes of receiving such awards, we may drop the bars and accept what we hear. Readers are much less affected by this motivation, naturally, because writers are not able to offer immediate rewards for acceptance of their ideas.

THE TALKER'S ADVANTAGE

Nonverbal communication is an important tool in the art of persuasion, and the bulk of its advantages falls, not to the writer, but the talker. Of course the writer has pictures, charts, diagrams, color, punctuation and various kinds of printing to bolster his written words, but all of these are meager compared with what is available to the talker. He confronts his listeners with a living scene that often has tremendous force. He can weep and moan;

threaten his listeners with a disdainful look that says, "Do what I say or you'll have regrets"; radiate contagious enthusiasm for the idea he wants accepted; speak in a cultured voice that lulls listeners out of any critical attitude, or simply confront his listeners with a smile that makes them feel good toward him.

The 1940 Presidential campaign, as studied by Columbia University's researchers, gives us a good example of how listeners are sometimes influenced almost solely by nonverbal communication. Strictly in terms of how the two candidates spoke, and not what they said, the researchers found that people in general were affected adversely by Wendell Willkie's speech manner and favorably by Franklin Roosevelt's.

Nonverbal communication offers the talker another advantage in persuasion seldom available to the writer. The talker can usually see his listeners. As a result he can watch their reactions as he proceeds with his arguments. If the listeners seem to be souring on what they hear, the talker can withdraw, replan his attack and return for another try. Or, right on the spot, he can shift his oral presentation until the listeners' reactions improve.

The Illinois oil salesman mentioned is a master at using the nonverbal reactions of his customers to time his persuasive sales arguments. Although he has driven across the state to see a client, the salesman may not say a word about oil to the man. "I can't always put my finger on what happens," says the salesman, "but I'll walk into a man's office, and before many minutes I'll sense how things are with him. He may not be quite so glad to see me as before. Perhaps he's more nervous than usual, opening mail, interrupting with phone calls or any of a number of things. I decide fast that this is not my day, so I make a hasty exit and plan to come back when things are better."

From the foregoing pages you may see that the force of persuasive speech depends upon a number of factors in addition to the content of the spoken words themselves. It is well that you are now aware of these factors, for it means that they will have less chance of affecting your critical abilities negatively. However, in the final analysis, it is the content of the talk that must be acted upon. To do this effectively the listener needs a knowledge of the techniques used in composing persuasive language.

In terms of content there are two broad types of persuasive talks:

The first type spreads out the facts, for and against the proposal that the speaker wants accepted by the listener. As he starts to talk the speaker may not reveal the position he takes in relation to the facts, but before finishing he states his position and appeals to his listener to take the same position.

The critical evaluation of such a talk is fairly simple, provided all the facts are heard and understood. Then it's a matter of weighing pros and cons and deciding if the facts for the proposal are more or less valid than the ones against it.

The second type of persuasive talk, however, does not make such an easy task out of critical evaluation. All the facts are not necessarily presented to the listener. Indeed, the talker may not lean too heavily on facts at all; he may depend upon emotion-arousing devices to move his listeners to accept his proposal. The man who uses these devices has usually declared allegiance to the proposal for which he speaks. To put across that proposal he may attempt to influence his listeners with or without ethical

133

consideration of his methods. In other words, the talker may resort to almost any workable persuasive technique so long as it produces the desired results.

LISTEN FOR SEVEN TECHNIQUES

Most of these techniques have been well defined by the Institute for Propaganda Analysis. The institute calls them "propaganda techniques," perhaps somewhat inaccurately according to the dictionary definition of the word "propaganda." However, the techniques are used by persuasive talkers, both in the trained-speaker category and in the conversational, person-to-person category. The institute has identified seven techniques and given them titles:

1. Name calling. As we know, people tend to summarize whole areas of their experience under labels. The labels, when heard, flood the listener with emotion, his mind stops working on a logical basis, and he may, without giving his decision careful thought, take the action desired of him by the persuasive talker. With this technique the labels are usually selected by the talker to produce a negative reaction in the listener against some thing, cause or person.

For example, the term "Communist" has been an emotion-laden label in America and has sometimes been devastatingly applied to people who have not been Communists.

2. Glittering generalities. This technique works in a fashion similar to the first one, but here the labels are likely to illuminate the talker's cause, or anything or anybody supporting it, in a favorable light. Examples of such labels are: freedom-loving, democratic, American, Christian, efficient, patriotic and friend. Such words often cause good feelings to fill the listener on an emotional level, and again he may make a decision to accept the speaker's proposition without reasoning it out.

A political candidate may be introduced as "that great, democratic, freedom-loving, patriotic American." In the face of these "glittering generalities" it's sometimes hard for a listener to believe otherwise.

3. *Transfer.* With this device the speaker frequently refers to sources of authority, prestige or reverence that his listener respects. He will not explicitly say that the sources support his cause, but he gives the impression that they do. Such sources might include a church, a highly respected civic organization, the flag, the will of the people or public education.

As the political candidate speaks he tells about attending church, belonging to civic groups, attending local schools and having respect for the will of the people. Many listeners are likely to make a "transfer," assuming that these things mentioned by the candidate all rally behind the man, even though he really does not say so.

4. *Testimonial.* In support of his cause the speaker employing this technique cites testimony from respected, well-known people, or he may call on them to give the testimony personally.

On the television screen a famous movie star appears, testifying to all the favorable mechanical features of a new-model car that is being advertised. Because the star is well known the noncritical listener fails to question how qualified the actor is to talk about technical factors in a car, and the actor's words persuade the listener to buy the vehicle without question.

5. *Plain folks.* As listeners we will often readily accept the word of a person who seems to be very much like us, while, on the other hand, we become suspicious of people who are different from us. The persuasive talker may take advantage of this inconsistency to sway his listeners by doing things to make himself appear to be one of them.

A well-dressed salesman visiting the foreman of a machine shop will remove his coat and necktie before entering the shop. Inside, he practically forces handshakes out of the grease-smeared workmen to show that he, like them, doesn't mind dirty hands, and he uses bad grammar mixed with considerable cursing because he figures that that is how the average shophand talks. If his outward change of character is accepted by the foreman, the salesman has a better chance to gain acceptance of what he says in his sales talk.

6. *Card stacking.* When a persuasive talker "stacks his cards" he edits his oral material in his own favor. Any evidence that supports his proposition will be spoken, but adverse evidence will be shrouded in silence.

"This vacuum cleaner," says the salesman, "has nine wonderful features." And he enumerates them, but he makes no reference to the disadvantages, of course. The noncritical listener accepts what he hears, failing to look beyond the spoken words for the full evidence.

7. *Band wagon.* This device appeals to follow-the-herd instincts that are strong in most of us. The persuasive speaker points out that many people are accepting his proposition, often leaving the listener with a feeling that he too should join the crowd.

The television announcer appears on the screen holding

a package of cigarettes. "Two billion of these were sold last year," he states. "Everyone is buying them. This year we expect to sell three billion or more." The announcer may give no solid evidence regarding the cigarettes' quality, but the listener, not exercising critical abilities, may buy the cigarettes simply because he understands that everyone else is buying them.

In addition to these seven devices there are, of course, other techniques used in oral persuasion. In their book, *General Speech*, A. Craig Baird and Franklin H. Knower point out a number of other things that persuasive talkers use or play upon to their advantage: "flattery; appeals to fear, hate, anger, frustration or discontent growing out of lack of opportunity or misfortune; the creation of devils on which to place blame; repetition and more repetition; wishful thinking, rationalization, rumor, distrust; identification with the great, the beautiful and the good; prophecies and positive suggestion."

IT CAN BE GOOD OR BAD

The persuasive techniques described over the last few pages may be put to good or bad uses, depending upon the causes for which they are made to work and how these causes affect the people who accept them. However, in the final analysis the listener must decide for himself whether oral persuasion should lead to accepting or rejecting the proposals presented. For his own good he should make his decisions by the use of logic. The persuasive techniques discussed above aim at getting listeners to bypass the areas of decision making where logic is applied; in other words, they try to get people to "jump to conclusions." But the critical listener does not jump to conclusions, because he takes time to test the oral evidence that he will use for accepting or rejecting what is being proposed to him.

The use of critical ability in aural communication does not mean challenging every word, phrase and sentence, because such mental activity would ruin comprehension, which lies at the very foundation of all listening. Therefore, as we talk about critical listening, it is important to keep in mind that comprehension must come first, with critical evaluation second.

When listening to persuasive speech, we find that the talker moves from one point of evidence to another, adding them all up in support of his over-all proposition. As each point is made the listener should concentrate upon it for the purpose of comprehension and then evaluate the point; by no means should he allow any single evaluation to become the final judgment of the entire talk—in other words, no *jumping to conclusions* before the end of a talk. For his final evaluation, the listener must wait until everything has been stated by the speaker. Even then, it is best if the listener can delay his acceptance or rejection of the speaker's proposal until after a cooling-off period during which his critical processes can operate under conditions less emotional than those encountered while listening.

TESTS TO APPLY

The actual critical process is best described as a testing of evidence—first as it is heard, a piece at a time, and then in its totality *after* it is heard. Below are four tests to which the evidence found in persuasive speech should be put.

1. Test of time

Evidence that was good yesterday is not necessarily valid today. The listener should try to determine the age of evidence that he hears. If it is old, it should be scrutinized more carefully than ever. A simple example: Government statistics of our economic situation a year ago might be completely worthless in terms of what is happening right now.

2. Test of the source's competency

Evidence is affected by the source from which it comes. Some people know what they are talking about; others don't, but talk just the same. A Hollywood actor may have much to say about an automobile, but this doesn't mean that he is a competent source for the information. The filling-station attendant down the street undoubtedly knows much more about automobiles. Statistics quoted by a talker may or may not be good, according to their source. If they come from the Federal government's Bureau of the Census, chances are that the statistics are good; but if they come from a small-scale survey made by the talker himself, they are less likely to be valid. The critical listener, therefore, must carefully consider the source of evidence that he hears.

3. Test of prejudice

This third test, perhaps the most important of all, has to do with the talker's neutrality, or lack of it, on the subject on which he speaks. The politician's evidence is likely to be affected by the desire for votes. The salesman's "facts" may be prejudiced by his desire to sell. There are many motives behind many people who talk to us, and these motives may prejudice their evidence. The critical listener must try to see what the talker stands to gain from people's acceptance of what he says.

4. Test of completeness

What a speaker doesn't say is important as a key to the motives behind his persuasion. If he verbally skirts certain points that should be included in his talk, these points, although not heard, become important. The critical listener should ask himself if the talker is leaving anything out of the oral discourse. If so, why does he leave it out? The listener may want to seek out that evidence before making any decision requested by the speaker. This might be accomplished through asking questions of the speaker, or, if that is not feasible, the listener might go to other sources to obtain the information. For example, a person, after listening to a salesman explain his product, might go to the consumer research publications for further information.

If the use of critical listening becomes more widespread in our culture, it will produce two results:

Life will be easier for the man who talks to persuade us to take action for our own good and for that of our fellow men.

The man who uses oral persuasion for less honorable reasons will find his task becoming increasingly difficult.

Chapter 12

Executives Must Listen

Management Development Associates of New York, which has as clients some of the nation's largest industries, recently asked the top executives of a large manufacturing plant in the Chicago area to survey the role that listening plays in their work. Later, Edward Walther, a partner of the management firm, went to the plant and at an executive seminar asked: "What do you think about this business of listening?" A series of discussions followed.

"Frankly, I had never thought of listening as an important subject by itself," said one man. "But now that I am aware of it, I think that perhaps 80 per cent of my work depends upon my listening to someone, or upon someone else listening to me."

"I've been thinking back about things that have gone wrong over the past couple of years," said another executive, "and I suddenly realize that many of the troubles have resulted from someone not hearing something, or getting it in a distorted way."

"It's interesting to me," said one man, "that we have considered so many facets of communication in the company, but have inadvertently overlooked listening. I've

141

about decided that it's the most important link in the company's communications, and it's obviously the weakest one."

THE AWAKENING TO LISTENING

These comments become part of an awakening that is taking place in a number of management circles across America. Business is hung together by its communication system. This communication, businessmen are frequently discovering, depends more upon the spoken word than upon the written word. The effectiveness of the spoken word depends upon how people listen.

In the business world men are saying that, above all, an executive must know how to listen.

Frank E. Fischer, an official of the American Management Association, points out that management has "talked too much and listened too little."

In a recent issue of the magazine *Nation's Business,* an article written about the basic skills that future industrial managers will need places listening at the top of the list.

The editors of *Fortune* magazine have been pointing out for a number of years that lack of listening is a major weakness in the business world.

When one such statement was made by *Fortune,* the Bureau of National Affairs polled 160 executives around the country in order to find how they felt about the magazine's contention. Ninety-six per cent of the executives agreed that management in general has failed to listen to people.

"All right," says the executive who has decided listening is important, "I am a bad listener. But what do I do about it?"

The answers to this question all too often are dreary

echoes of what we heard at school: "Pay attention!" "Open up your ears!" "Try to understand the other fellow!" "Keep an open mind!"

But these recommendations mean little to a busy executive. They indicate nothing about the skill of listening and give no concrete suggestions for its improvement. For the sister communication skills, reading, writing and speaking, ample literature and specific training programs are readily available to the executive, but for listening he has had practically nothing with which to work.

However, there are signs indicating that this situation is changing. Industrial-training people are developing programs for listening improvement.

Management Development Associates, mentioned before, is pioneering in listening training in the independent consultant field of executive improvement. The firm already offers specific training methods in listening.

Universities and special management-training schools are offering communication courses that include attention to the subject of listening. The American Management Association offers such training in New York.

A number of industrial firms have developed or are developing listening-improvement programs for their executives. General Electric Company and Western Electric Company, Inc., are two examples.

And there are signs that a considerable body of literature is developing to help management people with listening improvement. This book itself is one step toward building up that literature.

AWARENESS FIRST

A basic step for improving most skills is taken by building awareness of the skill's importance. The same holds true for training people to listen in business. This skill's importance, of course, varies from business to business, but there are a number of general areas where the need for good listening is universal.

On an elementary level, listening is important in the everyday communication of information. When people in businesses fail to hear and understand each other, the results are costly.

Not long ago in a major Midwestern industrial concern that manufactures parts for heavy machinery, an order from a customer was received by telephone. The order, once it was put into writing, stated that sixty machine parts of a particular kind were to be shipped to a firm almost 1,500 miles away. Each of the parts weighed nearly 100 pounds. They were crated and forwarded to the buyer by railroad freight.

Several days later a representative of the buying firm phoned the manufacturer. "What on earth is the idea?" he asked. "I sent a truck down to the freight depot to pick up your shipment. Before I knew it, our trucker was making several trips. I assumed he could do the job in one trip, but then I learned there were sixty crates waiting for him instead of the six I had ordered. Will you arrange immediately to get the extra ones out of here? They're using up valuable floor space."

The order had been received on the telephone by a man in the manufacturer's sales department. He had relayed the order orally to a person who wrote it down as sixty rather than six. The company paid for forwarding and returning fifty-four heavy crates and a valuable customer was irritated.

Here is another example of the cost of bad listening:

When a Long Island, New York, plant hired a number of new employees a few years ago to work over a forge used for heating tool steel, a meeting was held to instruct the men verbally in the use of grappling irons. The men used the irons, with removable wooden handles, to hold the steel in the forge. When a man finished with a hot grappling iron, the instructor carefully emphasized that he was to hang it on the wall to the right of the forge. As the irons cooled, they were to be moved to the left wall. And when an employee needed a grappling iron, he, of course, would take it from the left wall.

Shortly after the meeting an employee hung a hot grappling iron on the wrong wall. Another man walked into the room, reached up and grabbed the hot iron. The metal burned and stuck to the skin of his hand. Unable to let go, he fainted and fell, with the grappling iron still stuck to his hand. By the time the man was found, the burns were so serious that they impaired his ability to work for the remainder of his life.

At a hearing after the accident, the man who had placed the iron on the wrong wall swore that he hadn't heard anybody say hot irons were to be hung to the right of the forge. However, other employees testified to his presence when the instructions were given. Also, the instructor testified that the guilty man from all appearances had been listening intently while the instructions were given.

This kind of inefficient listening, if it could be tallied in terms of dollars and cents, undoubtedly costs the nation's industry millions of dollars a year. Not only does it cause expensive mistakes such as the two above, but it also creates a fear of the spoken word which in turn causes businessmen to write out even the simplest of communications.

If we move from the basic information-passing function of oral communication to its broader aspects in industry, we find that listening plays an increasingly important role.

As any industrial firm grows, horizontal communication from one division of the company to another becomes more of a problem to maintain. Each division becomes larger and at the same time, in many cases, more autonomous. Very often the growth of different divisions results in their actual physical separation. Purchasing is on one floor. Sales is on another floor. Engineering is in another building. Eventually the people in the different divisions get out of touch with one another. The situation often reaches the point where the people of one division do not even know those in another.

This kind of separation is a barrier to communication and it results, all too often, in the right hand's not knowing what the left is doing, even within a single company with a single purpose.

Of course, between widely separated divisions there is communication, but it often must flow from one division toward the top of a company and back down into another division. Or it may flow through a coordinating department that keeps in touch with all divisions. These communication routes serve purposes, but still the important people of different divisions do not really get acquainted with one another, and there is a stiffness of communication that dampens the flow of many useful ideas. On the other hand, when an effort is being made to bring the important people of different divisions together, they get acquainted, and a freedom of communication develops that can be a valuable asset to the entire company.

Here's an example of what can happen when personal oral communication has no way of flowing between separated divisions:

146

In a northern New York State firm manufacturing replacement parts for farm machinery, a man in the engineering department had an idea for making what he thought would be a valuable improvement on some of the company products. He suggested replacing cotter pins with lock rings on a number of parts. To the people of his department the idea seemed worthwhile and the changes it required seemed minor. The idea was put into writing and was circulated through other departments of the company. There were no objections, so the change was made.

When the first lock rings appeared on new parts, an executive in the sales department saw the change and ran to the firm's sales manager. "Good lord," he said, "who ever let this get through? Farmers are not going to like these lock rings. If they lose a cotter pin they can replace it with a nail or a piece of wire. If they lose one of these rings they'll be licked if another one isn't available."

As it turned out, the executive was right. Farmers objected to the change and the manufacturer eventually had to revert to cotter pins. The whole incident was costly, both in terms of making the changes and in terms of lost customers.

The executive who predicted the trouble said to me recently, "This place has become so large that I seldom meet up with an engineer. Information like that about the cotter pins often seems so insignificant that it gets lost in formal communication channels. But if we could sit down and just chew things over—and, of course, listen to each other—such problems would often be ironed out before they ever got started."

Of course many companies furnish opportunities for the personnel of different divisions to meet and "chew things over." One large company in the Midwest brings its superintendents from various divisions together one afternoon a week. Most of the superintendents are involved in manufacturing different things. Each weekly meeting begins on a formal basis, but later the men are encouraged to talk informally with each other while they have coffee.

"I'll be talking with a fellow I never knew before these meetings were held," said one of the superintendents recently, "and he'll start telling me about how he solved a problem over in his plant. Suddenly I'll wake up to the fact that he's talking about something that has been bothering me for a long time. By the time I've heard him out he's told me how to take care of my own problem."

Here's where listening becomes a valuable tool for the smoother functioning of industrial management. Emphasis can be placed on listening at formal meetings designed to strengthen horizontal communication; or at informal gatherings, such as in a company lunchroom where people from different divisions eat; or in routine, day-by-day contacts as they naturally occur between people in separate divisions. Awareness to the value of listening in such situations is the key.

UPWARD COMMUNICATION

As an industrial firm grows, and horizontal communication becomes difficult, problems also occur in a vertical direction. When men talk about industrial communication today, the terms "upward" and "downward" communication are often heard. When the top man says something to his subordinates, this is "downward" communication. When the process is reversed, it is "upward" communication.

In a small company these two avenues of communication

are fairly simple to control. The head man may even walk among all of his employees, talk with them and listen to what they have to say. But when a company grows large the two avenues become long and complicated. The distance, measured in numbers of people, between the top man and employees down below plays havoc with communication.

Downward communication has many mediums through which it can travel. There are sound systems for making announcements. Company magazines and newspapers are now flourishing, and the head men can use them for writing messages to employees. Management may write a message to employees, reproduce it and enclose a copy in each pay envelope. There are bulletin boards to convey messages downward. The top men can call meetings of employees and talk to them. Managers can give a message to subordinates with the order to "pass it on down." There are many ways of talking to employees. It has been estimated that industry in America spends well over $100,-000,000 a year on downward communication.

But with all the money spent, downward communication is a frustrating affair in most instances. The top man says something and through one avenue or another the communication goes downward—but then no answer comes back. It's similar to your talking to a person who doesn't react to you. The more you talk the more uncertain you become of what you are saying.

Upward communication in industry has few effective avenues on which to travel. There are suggestion boxes which pick up messages directed to the top. Meetings of employees are held, but it is difficult to encourage the employees to say what is really on their minds. The top management may conduct attitude surveys to find out what the employees are thinking about, but such surveys usually can't work on a continuing basis to record rapid changes in attitudes, and also the surveys must be exceptionally well conducted to be of real value.

There's one more avenue for upward communication to take, and at first glance it seems like the obvious avenue to use. It has direct communication lines from bottom to top that are operative all the time that business is carried on. The lines work like this: The man working at the bench talks to his foreman, the foreman talks to his superintendent, the superintendent to his boss, and, relayed from person to person, the information eventually reaches the top. Sounds like a good system, but it seldom works well because the people who form the human communication chain upward often do not know how to listen.

When there is poor listening, this avenue of upward communication fails for at least three reasons:

1. Without good listeners, people do not talk freely; therefore the flow of communication upward is seldom set into motion.
2. However, if the flow should start, only one bad listener is needed to stop the movement toward the top.
3. Even if the flow should continue to the top, the messages are likely to be badly distorted along the way.

THE BOSS FINDS IT HARD TO LISTEN

Poor listening habits may be brought into industry by employees who received no training at school in the skills of listening, but once the habits have arrived they may be intensified by the social structure of industry itself.

For example, a boss, because of his position in the chain

of command, may find it difficult to be a good listener when a subordinate is talking. Indeed, the boss may give lip service to his being a good listener by announcing, "My door is always open. Walk in any time." But in spite of the announcement his ears often remain closed to what is said by subordinates who accept the invitation.

In part, at least, this bad listening situation may result from a boss's assumptions about his position as a leader of men. In our society we talk about how leaders should understand the people under them; therefore leaders should listen. On the other hand, the leader is a man who "should be all-knowing," we say. In order to become a leader he should have all "the answers at his finger tips." If a man in a position of leadership feels strong about this concept, he is likely to find it difficult to listen to those below him. Inside himself he may fear that the act of listening will indicate weakness on his part, that as a person who should have all the answers he shouldn't have to listen.

THE MESSAGES ARE FILTERED

Another barrier to good listening in upward communication is that the upward chain of talkers and listeners contains what we have termed "emotional filters," and inevitably they cause distortion to messages.

"Nearly every man in an organization's chain of command has his ideas of how things should be run," said an official of Western Electric recently. "What the man hears is likely to be interpreted in light of these ideas."

Often without conscious recognition of the fact, listeners may accept, reject and change some of what they hear. In industry the social structure of an organization may even accentuate such listening distortion.

151

A foreman hears his men continually discussing a policy that has been put into effect by top management. The men consider the policy unfair. The foreman tries to pass the information upward, thinking that perhaps the policy can be reviewed and changed before a grievance action occurs. But somewhere along the line there's a man who is afraid that his boss won't want to be bothered with gripes coming from the men below. So he changes the message around a little to keep his boss from getting upset. Eventually the message, through such editing, gets turned completely around and top management hears that the policy is being accepted with open arms by all the men in the plant.

It would be absurd to assume that the lines of upward communication could be made to operate without hitches, but there is no reason to think that they cannot be improved.

If the people involved can be better listeners, if they can understand the importance of listening, the lines of communication will be improved. More and better listening on the part of top management is especially vital to encourage improvement all down the line.

LISTENING IRONS OUT PROBLEMS

And here we touch upon an important by-product of improved listening on the part of management.

"I try to get our foremen to simply sit down, shut up and listen to their men when problems arise," said the top superintendent of a large Indiana manufacturing plant recently. "I learned from hard experience that listening can be an asset.

"A man will come into your office wanting to talk about

something. He has a problem on his mind that's been bothering him for several days.

"Now, if you can let him talk, no interruptions, just let him go, you can almost bet that he'll walk out of your office without a problem. You won't have to say much either. As the fellow talks, he'll slowly show himself what the answer to the problem is, or he might find that he doesn't even have a problem.

"Other times a man will strut up to you. He's mad. He objects to this and he can't stand that. If you start arguing with him, trying to defend yourself or someone else, the man may go away, but he'll still be mad, and probably he'll be back with the same objections turned into monsters.

"In the same situation if you can get hold of yourself and hear the man out, try to understand him, his objections will very often vanish into thin air. They either didn't exist to begin with, or the man discovers as he talks that the objections are so minor that he shouldn't even be bothering with them."

Dr. Arthur Kellner, a New York industrial psychologist, explains, "When a person with a problem talks to someone who does not listen, his 'self-concept' is challenged and his problem becomes more acute. However, when such a person can talk to an interested listener, his 'self-concept' is preserved, or even enhanced, and he goes away feeling better."

People all up and down the line of industrial organizations need to be heard; they need to feel free to talk to their superiors and be met with sympathetic understanding. This requires, on the part of superiors, a measure of what we call "nondirective" listening. The listener hears, tries to understand (and later shows the understanding by taking action if it's required); but during an oral discourse, the listener refrains from firing his own thoughts back at the person talking.

LABOR AND MANAGEMENT LISTEN

This kind of listening has even led to improved labor relations between management and unions.

One large industrial firm in Indiana has seen grievance actions practically disappear in the past couple of years.

"We used to meet with union representatives only when there was a need for a meeting," said an official of this firm. "Those meetings were only called for a reason, and the reason usually meant there was trouble.

"A couple of years ago, we decided to ask the union representatives to meet with us regularly, reason or no reason. Today we have an informal get-together about once a week. Often there is nothing specific on the agenda. We only sit and talk. I think that in these relaxed meetings we've learned to listen to each other. If there's a problem on the horizon it gets aired by one party or the other. More times than not these problems seem to disappear as we talk. And they're the kind of problems that used to grow into grievances. Now, I think we've only had one grievance in about eighteen months."

Nondirective listening also gives talkers a chance to do something they seldom have the opportunity of doing otherwise. When a problem appears in a person's mind it may be unrealistic, but a man can't find this out unless he can step away from the problem and take a look at it. Being able to talk freely to someone gives him such an opportunity. A listener who simply acts as a sounding board offers the talker a chance to hear himself expressing his problem. Often this very act helps him see his problem in its true light.

Making a good nondirective listener out of every person in an industry, from shop foreman to chairman of the board, is nearly impossible. However, many people in management can be made aware of nondirective listening, how it works and where its value lies. Also, key people can be given training in nondirective listening; such training is already being offered to employees in some firms—Western Electric, for example. Efforts in this direction are almost certain to reduce the everyday frictions that burden industry.

GOOD LISTENERS SAVE DOLLARS

Another by-product that can come from improved listening in business might be called "economy of communication."

Incidents created by poor listening cause businessmen to have a real fear of oral communication. As a result, they insist that more and more communication be put into writing. Naturally, a great deal of communication in business needs to be concise and to be a part of the record. But this pressure to write is often carried too far. The smallest detail becomes "memoed." Paperwork piles higher and higher, and it causes part of the tangle that we call "red tape."

Writing and reading, to begin with, are much slower processes than speaking and listening.

Writing and reading in business require more personnel, more equipment and more space than do speaking and listening. Often a stenographer is involved, and also a messenger to carry the written communications. Dictating machines, typewriters and other writing materials are needed. And finally, few people ever feel it is safe to throw away a written communication, at least for several weeks or months; so filing equipment is needed, along with someone to do the filing.

In the oral situation there are more human senses at work than in the visual. Therefore, if there's good listening, more can be communicated in one message. And perhaps most important of all, there is the give-and-take feature of oral communication. If the listener doesn't understand a message, he can straighten matters out then and there.

In any business today the economy factor in oral communication is forced to work at times. The head of a large company's estimating department expressed this fact as he talked to me recently.

"In our department," he said, "we have written procedures for just about everything we do. But every few days we get a rush job. A salesman is closing a deal out in the field. He needs a fast price estimate on a piece of equipment that he's about to sell.

"Well, when that happens, we are forced to drop all of our written procedures. We grab telephones and run here and there in the plant to talk with different people. The paperwork on such a rush job may not catch up with us for several days."

In rush situations oral communication often works well because people are highly motivated to listen and automatically do it better. If, through listening improvement, the same kind of oral communication could be used in more routine operations, there is no doubt of the savings it would make for industry.

RAPID CHANGE REQUIRES GOOD LISTENING

More rapid communication makes a contribution in another respect.

Innovation in today's industry sometimes moves at a fantastic speed. The machine that was new last week is ready to be replaced with a better one this week. The customer who is satisfied with a product today is suddenly enticed away by a competitor who has quickly produced a new and better product.

To keep up with this pace, men in industry have to learn fast. Often the things they need to know are not written down because there has been no time to do the writing. Oral communication is the kind that can keep up with such a pace if any kind of communication can. But again, listeners are needed.

A man partially responsible for developing farm machinery parts in a large firm said to me recently:

"We went into this business after the war. As we looked into the farm-machinery field we found that things were spurting ahead in a developmental way. It was difficult to get to the forefront of the field, because hardly anything had been written down that you could really call up-to-date. In the beginning we were faced with the problem of how and where to get our information.

"After discussing the problem, we decided there was only one approach and we took it. We went out into the farm-machinery field and listened. For instance, we attended all the association meetings visited by farm-machinery people. I would rent a suite of hotel rooms, bring in food and drink, and then ask important people to drop around. Often in a hotel room we would have engineers from the farm-machinery manufacturers and important people from a number of universities. They would start talking over their problems. Usually they'd be talking about farm-machinery developments that were needed at the moment or ones that would be important in the near future. We seldom said a word, but just listened. Sometimes we'd be still listening at four the next morning, but, frankly, that's where we got our know-how to build the business we have today."

Technological know-how, gained in a hurry, is crucial to modern business. But at the same time, as industrialists are becoming increasingly aware, another kind of knowledge is even more important to their existence; that is, a basic understanding of man.

PROGRESS THROUGH TEAMWORK

We consistently astound ourselves with what we can do technologically. In almost every field of industry we are making rapid progress toward what seems like perfection in a materialistic sense, toward the more perfect machine, more perfect building, and economic structure. The progress, however, seldom comes through individual efforts; it depends more and more upon men working with men as a team.

The "team" concept is important certainly, but it is worthless unless there's human understanding among the participants. Many management-training courses are directed toward the building of such understanding. They, in a sense, are trying to teach the humanities which were brushed over by many management people in their haste to understand the materialistic things of their world.

Whatever can be done to improve listening skill on the job will play a part in fostering the human understanding necessary for any team success. Listening is a phase of personal communication that gets close to the core of a human being to seek a basis for understanding.

IMPROVEMENT CAN BE MADE

Essentially there are two steps that lead to listening improvement in industry: (1) building awareness of the importance of listening in any given industrial situation, and (2) developing experience in the kind of listening required.

Often in an industrial firm, there are time and facilities available for taking only the first step, that of building awareness. The first step, however, has the potential for improving listening to a surprising degree.

Listed below are sixteen suggestions that might be put into effect by management-training people in building a listening program. Some of the suggestions are designed for developing awareness and are found mostly at the top of the list. Other suggestions are aimed at providing listening experience that can be helpful to people in industry. The suggestions have been drawn from the work of people active in the management-development field, and from my own thinking while working with people in the field of business and industrial management.

1. Devote an executive seminar, or seminars, to a discussion of the role and function of listening as a management tool.

2. If possible, bring in qualified speakers and ask them to discuss listening with special reference to how it might apply to management. (Speakers are available at a number of universities where listening is being taught as a part of communication training.)

3. Assign individuals to read, digest, and report on specific articles on listening. (Many of this book's chapters furnish pertinent material for such reading; the bibliography at the end suggests other selected items; and a survey of current journals concerned with industrial training will readily produce still further materials.)

4. Ask management people to inventory their listening on the job. Provide them with a simple form divided

into spaces for each hour of the day. Each space is further divided to allow the user to keep track of the amount of time spent in reading, writing, speaking and listening. The form might be filled out by an executive himself, or perhaps by his secretary if she is in a position to observe most of his communication activities. At a later time, discuss the results of these forms after the communication times have been totaled. What percentage of the time do people spend listening? What might improved listening mean in terms of executive effectiveness?

5. Through a seminar, or a questionnaire designed for the purpose, ask executives to think of incidents in the past that were affected directly by the way people listened. Are there examples in which bad listening has caused trouble and good listening has produced exceptional results?

6. Ask executives to rate themselves as listeners. Provide a questionnaire based on the listening skills described in this book. Questions might be answered simply by "yes" or "no." Some of the questions might be as follows:

a. As people talk to you, do you find it difficult to keep your mind on the subject at hand, to keep from taking mental excursions away from the line of thought that is being conveyed?

b. Do you listen primarily for facts, rather than ideas, when someone is speaking?

c. Do certain words, phrases or ideas so prejudice you against a speaker that you cannot listen objectively to what is being said?

d. When you are puzzled or annoyed by what someone says, do you try to get the question straightened out immediately, either in your own mind or by interrupting the talker?

e. If you feel it would take too much time and effort to understand something, do you go out of your way to avoid hearing about it?

f. Do you deliberately turn your thoughts to other subjects when you believe a speaker will have nothing particularly interesting to say?

g. Can you tell by a person's appearance and delivery that he won't have anything worthwhile to say?

h. When somebody is talking to you, do you try to make him think you are paying attention when you are not?

i. When you are listening to someone, are you easily distracted by outside sights and sounds?

j. If you really want to remember what someone is saying, do you try to write down most of his discourse?

For all these questions, the answers should be "no" if the person is a good listener.

7. Give a test on listening ability to executives and show them the scores they make. There is at least one standardized test for this purpose, the Brown-Carlsen Listening Comprehension Test.* Discuss the meanings of the scores with the individuals tested.

8. Pair up executives, who work with each other, as "listening partners." Ask each man to evaluate his partner's listening ability over a period of time. Hold a discussion about what is found from these evaluations.

* *Published by the World Book Company, Yonkers-on-Hudson, New York.*

9. Ask executives to survey their letter writing over a short period of time to see if some of the written communication could be handled orally. If a man finds he is writing down much material that he could transmit orally, ask him to try to discover why he feels it necessary to write such communication.

10. Build up a library of spoken-word records of literature, speeches, etc., and make them available in a room that has a record player. Also lend the records to executives who might wish to take them home to enjoy at leisure. For such a library, material pertinent to the executive's work might be recorded so that interested people could listen for educational purposes.

11. Record a number of actual briefing sessions that may be held by plant superintendents or others. When new people go to work for the company, ask them to listen to these sessions as part of their initial training. Check their comprehension of what they hear by means of brief objective tests. Emphasize that this is being done because listening is important on the men's new jobs.

12. Get permission to record an actual conference held in the company. During a training session, ask the trainees to listen and then discuss the part that listening played or failed to play in the conference.

13. Instead of asking executives to read "must" articles that may appear in trade journals or technical publications, record the material and ask executives to listen to it.

14. Set up "role playing" situations wherein executives are asked to cope with complaints comparable to those they might hear from subordinates. Ask observers of the role playing to comment on how well an executive seems to listen. Do his remarks reflect that he has done a good job of listening? Does he keep himself from becoming emotionally involved in what the subordinate says? Does the executive do things that would encourage the subordinate to talk freely?

15. Frequently bring executives from different divisions together at informal meetings where they may talk and listen to each other freely. Perhaps one day a week the executive's lunchroom could be organized so that men who ordinarily do not get together will be seatmates.

16. If budgets and space allow, bring in lecturers on interesting subjects for evening meetings. Invite executives and their families to hear the speakers. Such lecture programs could be an integral part of the firm's listening-improvement activities.

Chapter 13

The Salesman: Fast Talker or Fast Listener?

It's one of our occupational diseases that's hard to cure once you're stricken," said a man to me not long ago.

The disease: talking too much. The occupation: salesman.

For many of us, the word "salesman" brings to mind an image of a nattily dressed individual who talks as though he had been "vaccinated with a phonograph needle." He sells iceboxes to Eskimos; and if you don't beware, he will sell you something you don't want.

The personality accounting for this image is disappearing from the scene, but many a salesman clings to the notion that one of his most valuable attributes is the ability to verbalize. He may recommend the "low-pressure sell," but we still find him cultivating his voice for purposes of oral persuasion. Books on how to talk are well read in the sales field, and adult-education courses on public speaking are almost certain to be well populated with salesmen. Deep inside many people who live by selling lies the conjecture that glibness has magic.

High-pressure salesmanship, however, is rapidly giving

way to low-pressure methods in the selling of both in-dustrial and consumer goods. Today's salesman is likely to center his attention upon the "customer-problem ap-proach" of vending his wares.

PERSUASION BY LISTENING

To put this approach to work, the skill of listening be-comes a valuable tool for the salesman, while vocal agility is less important. *How* a salesman talks becomes relatively unimportant because *what* he says, when it is guided by his listening, gives power to the spoken word.

There are a number of ways in which listening plays a role in the art of sales persuasion, and before going into them it might be pointed out that these listening attributes apply not only to persons labeled "salesmen" but also to many other people. Most of us frequently work at the art of persuasion. We try to persuade people to hire us. Pro-posals for marriage have to be made. We want someone to do us a favor or accept our ideas. In all such instances, the skill of listening is an asset.

Basic to any successful salesman is the fact that he likes people. If he doesn't, his selling career is probably a short one. Of course when you like people you are likely to listen to them. But what if you have difficulty liking peo-ple? The answer to this question might touch on a number of psychological factors, but I am certain that in most in-stances a positive approach to the problem can be taken through the medium of listening.

If you do a genuine job of listening, asking questions and listening to the answers, you will begin to put yourself in the other fellow's shoes. Through such listening you begin to develop *empathy*, which, by dictionary definition, means "mental entering into the feeling and spirit of a

165

person." When this happens, you are on the way to finding a more "common ground" with other people.

But while listening helps the salesman develop his good feelings toward customers, it also becomes a valuable tool in sales persuasion, in molding the customers' feelings toward the salesman.

HEARING WHAT IS WANTED

On a simple level, listening can serve as a means of learning customers' needs and problems in relation to what they want to buy or are going to be asked to buy.

"One big difficulty with new, inexperienced sales clerks is that they don't listen," John J. McGrath, manager of training for Macy's department stores in the New York area, told me.

"Here's what an inexperienced clerk often does: a customer steps to the counter and says, 'I want that blouse on display there. I'd like size 14 with short sleeves.' The clerk hears only: 'Blouse on display. Size 14.' She rushes away and brings back a blouse, size 14, but with long sleeves. The customer again explains, 'Short sleeves.' Back goes the clerk, and again the customer waits.

"In a store the size of ours, such incidents can run into money. There's useless work for the clerk, unnecessary handling of merchandise and, more important, possibly an irritated customer. That's why in our training we stress, 'Listen before you act.' "

The "listen-before-you-act" approach to selling is built around a central question: How can a person sell either himself or his product if he doesn't know what the prospective buyer wants?

This premise is simple enough, but it still remains unrecognized by many who sell.

I recently undertook a survey of 100 housewives to learn their reactions to retail salespersons. The women were not asked to comment on listening ability, but a large percentage of their remarks reflected directly upon the listening factor in sales. Here are a few of the housewives' statements.

Favorable comments:

"The salesperson recognizes that I have a problem, and seems to express eagerness and willingness to help me even if she cannot."

"She says substantially this, occasionally: 'I know what you want. We do not have it. We do have something which might help you. I am not sure. Would you like to look at it?'"

"She remembers me and calls me by name."

Unfavorable comments:

"When I enter the store, one member of a group of chatting clerks leaves the group to wait on me. As I start to state my needs, she turns back to deliver one more remark to the group she just left."

"The salesman listens to my statement of needs with obvious boredom—wordlessly—and with a shrug turns to secure the requested article."

"The salesperson refuses to 'hear me out.' Before I can finish stating my needs, this 'eager beaver salesman' starts delivering a memorized sales talk."

The importance of listening in selling has been further demonstrated through a survey completed by a large retail-stores organization. The survey, as reported by Cedric Adams, columnist for the *Minneapolis Star*, was aimed at discovering why the stores lost customers. The results should be of interest to every retailer.

They showed that 1 per cent of lost customers die; 3 per cent move away from where the stores are located; 4 per cent just naturally float from one store to another; 5 per cent change stores upon their friends' recommendations; 9 per cent switch stores because they can buy cheaper elsewhere; 10 per cent are "chronic beefers"; and *68 per cent stop buying at the stores because the sales personnel are indifferent to their needs!*

RESEARCH BY LISTENING

It becomes increasingly obvious that the efficient salesman is a person who first, in a sense, researches his customers by listening to them. In the beginning, he listens for two words that are all important to future relations with any customer: the person's name. Then the salesman listens to discover the customer's needs and problems that can be fulfilled by whatever the salesman may have to offer.

Oddly enough, many business organizations are paying large sums of money to have the same type of research job done by specialists in the field of public opinion. These specialists, many of whom are psychologists with years of training in how to understand people, make carefully prepared surveys of people to learn about their motivations for buying. From the reports made by these researchers businessmen receive guidance in making products and designing sales methods that fit in with customers' motivations.

While businessmen are spending money on motivational-research specialists, who are usually well worth their costs, the research potential of the company's sales

force is often overlooked. At the finger tips of every salesman is the opportunity to learn a certain amount about
customer motivation. The method? Careful development of
their ability to listen.

The salesman should never cease his aural study of
people who buy or fail to buy from him. As these people
talk he should note with care both what they say and what
they do *not* say. The latter activity was discussed earlier in
the book as "listening between the lines," an important
ingredient of listening concentration. This skill becomes
important because few customers put their *real* objections
to a product into spoken words. However, the way they
orally skirt an objection may reveal what the objection is
if the listener is looking beyond the content of what he
hears. When the salesman uses his listening skills in such
ways he has an opportunity to learn about customer motivations.

If a company's salesmen will listen to customers, and if
the firm's management will listen to the salesmen, the
company, in a sense, maintains an open ear to the public's
desires. It's an ear that can listen continually to catch
changes in public sentiment that might have an effect on
the company.

IT GIVES THE CUSTOMER A CHANCE

In addition to its use as a tool for learning about customers, the skill of listening is an asset to sales persuasion
in other ways.

John Zeiger, a New York management consultant who
has worked in marketing, says: "A salesman, in his eagerness to sell, often forgets a basic fact about the sales situation: The salesman wants action on the part of the customer; he wants the customer to buy. But in forgetting

this fact, many salesmen take all the action and leave no room for action on the part of the customer. The man who listens leaves room for action by the customer. In fact, the listening will even help initiate the action."

From my own encounters with salesmen I can draw examples of what Zeiger is talking about.

One time I was approached by a young insurance salesman who knew that I was interested in buying life insurance. As we began to talk, I was about to ask him some questions about insurance that had been on my mind.

"But if you'll let me start from the beginning," he said, "your questions will be answered by what I say."

The young man then launched into what sounded to me like a prepared speech. Soon he was taking more time than I felt willing to give him and he still hadn't answered my questions. I even tried to stop him, to get answers to my questions and perhaps to buy his insurance, but my interruptions seemed to bother him. I guess he felt that I was interfering with his sale. By the time he finished talking I was late for an appointment, irritated with him, and in no mood to buy insurance.

By listening to what a customer has to say, the salesman allows the customer's interest to develop in a way that is pertinent to the customer himself. Many times the person will talk himself into buying something, with hardly a word from the salesman.

OBJECTIONS SHOULD BE HEARD

A problem faced by every salesman is what to do when he meets objections made by a customer. Usually there's a natural inclination to argue, to defend the product that's for sale. Successful salesmen who have learned from hard experience usually refrain from countering objections with arguments, but many others fall into the trap. Indeed there are even sales organizations that encourage such defensive action by providing their salesmen with statements to meet various objections.

A college student a few summers ago considered selling Bibles during his summer vacation. After visiting the Bible sales organization, he showed me a mimeographed set of instructions. One section of the instructions was labeled: "How to meet customer objections." At the top of the list was one anticipated customer objection:

"I just can't afford a Bible."

The answering statement for the salesman was worded like this:

"You say you can't afford a Bible! But I see that you have a television set [radio, phonograph, etc.]. I am sure you wouldn't put your own personal luxuries before spiritual matters. Probably you bought these luxury items on time payments. I want to point out that we offer this Bible through the same kind of financial arrangements."

Theoretically, such a statement would hit the customer so hard that he wouldn't dare do anything but buy a Bible. Perhaps the statement works on some customers, but to me it amounts to saying: "You're a heathen if you don't buy this Bible." I doubt if a salesman can make such insinuations and then expect very many people to buy the product for sale.

Men who have learned their salesmanship well find that one of the best ways to overcome objections is to take an interest in the objections—*to listen to them.* By listening carefully, the salesman may, first of all, fully understand the objection, an important requirement if he expects to make an intelligent statement concerning the objection. But also—and this is perhaps a more important function of sales listening—if the customer's arguments are weak, he may find that out for himself if he is allowed to talk freely.

AND SOMETIMES COMPLAINTS VANISH

A lubrication engineer who sells in Texas for a large oil company told me how he has learned to handle customer complaints.

"It used to be that when I got a complaint about our lubrication," he said, "I would rush to the customer's office armed with facts and figures, anything that I could get my hands on to defend our lubricants. I'd frequently prove that the lubricant wasn't at fault, but I did untold damage in the process. My proof would sometimes leave the customer feeling about three inches tall, and in Texas you don't do that to a fellow very often.

"Now when a customer complaint comes in, I go see the fellow and let him talk all he wants. Nine times out of ten his complaint vanishes."

One day the engineer was told to drive immediately to a certain manufacturing plant and see the purchasing agent. The engineer arrived to find the purchasing agent boiling over.

"That new barium grease you talked me into buying is about to wreck our plant," he barked at the engineer. "A conveyor belt was shaking itself to pieces because of what the grease has done to a bearing."

"Our grease?" asked the engineer.

"What else could it be? We just got the stuff in here this month. We haven't had bearing trouble for eighteen months at least. That other grease never gave us any trouble. The last bearing failure we had came from some grease monkey who'd been goofing off."

172

The purchasing agent continued in this vein, but then he suddenly stopped, picked up the telephone and called someone.

"Who's greasing that conveyor?" he asked. There was a pause. "Who? Wait a minute, I'm coming down."

The purchasing agent left his office for a few minutes. Upon returning, he said to the engineer, "Okay, it's all settled. It turns out to be more grease-monkey trouble. Sorry for getting you over here. Matter of fact, I just learned that the barium grease—where it gets used—is doing a terrific job."

KNOWING THE PRODUCT

Besides knowing customers and their problems, the successful salesman naturally must know his product. Studying the product itself is one way, but the salesman should not overlook possibly his most important of all sources for product information: the experience of the buyers and users. And how better can this source be tapped than through careful listening?

The sales executives in a firm manufacturing farm-machinery parts discovered the value of listening for picking up knowledge about their own products.

"Several times a year," one of the executives told me, "we travel in the field with our sales representatives, not to sell but to get ideas of how our products are being used. We spend most of the time listening to customers talking about their own businesses. We often pick up new ideas and uses for our current products. Not long ago, for example, a customer in Wisconsin solved a problem through a new application of one of our older products. When we visited him, he told us about what had happened and gave us permission to tell our other customers about the new use of the product. We've already made a number of sales as a result of what we heard up there in Wisconsin."

It has been reported that some 80 per cent of sales made by wholesalers and manufacturers' representatives are made only after the salesmen have called at least five times upon their customers. The earlier calls can always be more fruitful if they become "listening visits." Besides picking up valuable information regarding both products and customers, a salesman is also exercising a kind of persuasion that puts a friendly but firm pressure upon the prospective buyer. The customer begins to feel an obligation to give the salesman a hearing and to wonder if perhaps the salesman, because he listens well, hasn't learned enough to offer some useful counsel. When a man is in this frame of mind, the so-called "sales pitch" is hardly needed anymore.

EXERCISES FOR SALES LISTENING

Below is a list of nine suggestions designed to build awareness of the value of listening in sales and to provide experience in listening as it is applicable to selling. Some of the suggestions may be useful to individuals while others are more applicable to group sales training.

1. Divide a notebook up into sections, one for each customer. After making a call, write down all the information received aurally from the customer. As the information grows, refer to it before each return visit to a customer.

2. If at all possible, salespeople should listen to their own sales talks. A tape recorder beneath a counter might be used to record a retail salesclerk, for instance. There should be no element of "eavesdropping"; the recorder

should be used only at the volition of the salesperson himself and the recording should be heard only by persons selected by him. People in other sales fields, where recording actual talks is impossible, might orally reenact a sales interview and record it. Hearing one's self in the act of selling may often point up the need for more listening in the process.

3. Where a sales organization has a number of friendly customers, invite some of the more articulate ones to join salesmen in a group discussion of sales techniques. How do the customers feel about talking and listening on the part of salesmen? Try to get the customers to make critiques of the salesmen, and really listen to what they have to say.

4. Devote a sales meeting to the subject of listening. If possible bring in an outside speaker on the subject. Open the meeting up to a discussion of listening in relation to sales. A purchasing agent, provided he is articulate, might be willing to present his thoughts on the subject to a sales meeting.

5. Inventory listening and talking on sales calls over a period of time. After each call, estimate the percentages of time spent listening and talking to the customer. Average the percentages at the end of the period. How does the average of talking compare with that of listening?

6. Ask salesmen to rate their own listening abilities. Also give them a listening comprehension test. Methods for these two activities are discussed in the sixth and seventh suggestions found at the end of the previous chapter.

7. When "role playing" is used in sales training, tape-record the sessions. Listen to the recordings, paying special attention to what they reflect about listening on the part

of people playing salesmen's roles. Do the salesmen give customers a chance to speak freely? Do their remarks reflect that they have listened well to prior statements from customers?

8. As often as possible hold "bull sessions" among salesmen. In setting up these sessions, stress the fact that the participants can learn a great deal from each other if they give special attention to listening.

9. Install a record library. Also record important reading material for salesmen. For methods see the tenth and thirteenth suggestions at the end of the previous chapter.

Chapter 14

Why Conferences Need Good Listeners

Several thousand women left their homes today to sit in committee meetings at their clubs. Untold thousands of businessmen spent a large part of the day in conferences. People in Washington, D.C., sat around tables trying to solve important problems that affect us all. Teachers in thousands of schools met to discuss how our children are being educated. And doctors in large numbers met in conferences concerning our health.

The world's most important affairs are conducted around conference tables. Many times, because of poor listening, the affairs are not conducted too well.

Richard Beckhard, executive director of Conference Counselors in New York, sometimes asks his clients to engage in a demonstration to illustrate one important factor that prevents conferences from functioning as well as they should. In a training conference for his clients, Beckhard will enforce a simple rule for perhaps ten or fifteen minutes.

"Directly after each man finishes talking," he explains, "let's maintain a thirty-second period of silence before another man speaks." Beckhard takes out a stop watch and his client-conferees start a discussion.

As the first participant finishes speaking, Beckhard raises a hand as a signal for silence. In thirty seconds he lowers his hand and the next participant to get the group's attention says what is on his mind. This procedure continues until the end of the demonstration.

During each interval of silence it's interesting to watch the conference participants. Most of them become tense, leaning forward in their chairs with their eyes fixed on Beckhard's raised hand. Toward the end of each thirty-second period of silence, the conferees make false starts, blurting out a word or two, or waving a hand to get attention. At the end of the thirtieth second, several people are likely to speak at once, and only after some confusion does one person gain the chance to speak alone.

After the demonstration, Beckhard asks the people to describe how they felt during the imposed periods of silence. Nearly everyone agrees that it was a hard thing to take. For many people, in fact, the thirty-second wait seemed painful.

A great many people at conferences are strongly motivated by an urge to influence the meeting by orally presenting their own views. When something stands in their way—like the period of silence—it often creates tension in the participants. People seldom display a strong urge to listen at conferences.

HOW MANY SHOULD BE LISTENING?

This badly deviated flow of oral communication is a serious matter to anyone conducting a meeting. The underlying principle of a successful conference requires both talking and listening. Each person in a conference should contribute his viewpoint, knowledge and experience to the group, which then seeks the best of all the conferees' thinking to solve the common problem. However, if there is far more talking than listening, the oral contributions are hardly worth the breath required to produce them.

As a matter of fact, at any given moment in a conference much more listening is required than speaking. In a meeting of five men, for example, at least four times more listening than talking is needed, because when one man is speaking four should be listening. In a ten-man conference, nine times more listening than talking is required—and so on.

How obvious the need for listening at conferences seems after only a few minutes of thinking about it. Indeed, it is so simple that we seem to have developed a can't-see-the-forest-for-the-trees complex about listening on these occasions. A great deal is being said and written about the subject of how to talk at a conference, how to compromise, how to get problem-centered, how to cope with certain types of individuals—and all of these can be very important—but too frequently the experts forget to say, "First and foremost you must learn how to listen at a conference!"

A good example of this forgetfulness shows up in a U.S. Government publication on how to conduct conferences. It was printed for a branch of the armed services, but it has also been distributed widely outside of the government. In thirty pages of text and illustrations, the term "listen" doesn't appear once!

On the other hand, of course, a number of authorities in the field recognize the need for listening, and stress it.

The late Irving J. Lee, in his book *How to Talk with People* as well as in a number of articles, frequently pointed up the importance of listening to each other when we meet to solve our mutual problems.

179

The famous semanticist S. I. Hayakawa says:

"If a conference . . . is to result in the exchange of ideas, we need to pay particular heed to our listening habits. . . . Living in a competitive culture, most of us are most of the time chiefly concerned with getting our own views across, and we tend to find other people's speeches a tedious interruption of the flow of our own ideas. Hence, it is necessary to emphasize that listening does not mean simply maintaining a polite silence while you are rehearsing in your mind the speech you are going to make the next time you can grab a conversational opening. Nor does listening mean waiting alertly for the flaws in the other fellow's arguments so that later you can mow him down. Listening means trying to see the problem the way the speaker sees it—which means not sympathy, which is *feeling* for him, but empathy, which is *experiencing with* him. Listening requires entering actively and imaginatively into the other fellow's situation and trying to understand a frame of reference different from your own. This is not always an easy task."

Effective listening during a conference is not easy, for it means that practically all the listening factors discussed in this book come frequently into play. Let us see how some of these factors apply.

THE AURAL GENERATION OF IDEAS

At one point we talked about how listening controls the flow of oral information. Good listening habits produce a free movement of information, while poor ones hinder the flow by causing talkers to take actions that do not make for efficient communication. With good listeners the talker will often open up and say more clearly what he has on his mind. With poor listeners he will sometimes withdraw partially or completely and not say exactly what he means; or he may turn his thinking away from the conference problem to the problem of making the other people understand some small point that he struggles to get across.

A friend of mine was stationed in the Pacific after World War II. He was a second lieutenant in an Air Force communication center with a colonel as the chief communication officer. One time the lieutenant was asked by the colonel to represent him in a staff meeting of high-ranking officers at the Air Force headquarters building. The lieutenant was the lowest-ranking officer at the meeting.

After considerable discussion among the other officers the lieutenant felt he had two contributions to make to the conference, and he started to talk. As he made his first point there seemed to be a wavering of attention among the higher-ranking officers. The lieutenant struggled harder and harder to get across the fairly simple point he was trying to make. Finally he gave up and said no more during the whole meeting. What he had wanted to say would not have taken more than a minute to express. As it was, he talked several minutes and still didn't say very much of what he had intended.

Such lack of listening attention keeps many a conference working at a low level of efficiency. Good ideas are blocked from entering into the group thinking process, and large amounts of time and energy may be spent by people overworking their vocal cords expressing even the poorest ideas.

LISTENING MAKES LISTENERS

Besides helping a conferee to express himself in an efficient fashion, listening to his talk will often induce him to be a better listener when others are talking. Listening, in a sense, is contagious. You listen to me, and I begin to develop an obligation to listen to you.

Perhaps you have seen someone use the foregoing fact to advantage at a conference. In the beginning the person remains quiet, listening carefully to the other conferees as they talk and talk. Finally, after the others have run down somewhat, the silent one speaks. The other conferees suddenly pay attention to him in a way they never did with each other, for they feel obligated to him. At this point the belated speaker may exert the strongest influence of anyone in the room.

When several members of a conference put emphasis on listening at the start of a meeting, there is likely to be a general improvement of listening among all the conferees. A conference leader should take advantage of this fact. By his own example of good listening habits, and by calling the conferees' attention to the need for listening, the conference leader may often produce listening improvement throughout the group. Of course a conference leader, more than anyone else, *should* set a good listening example. He needs to grasp what is said even more than anyone else; otherwise he can hardly fulfill the requirements of a good leader.

CONCENTRATION ON GROUP THINKING

At another point in the book the skill of aural concentration was discussed. In conferences, aural concentration means concentrating not only upon the words of one conferee at a time, but also upon the general line of thought that the group as a whole is taking toward whatever task it is trying to accomplish.

The mental ingredients which aid aural concentration, as you remember, were four in number: (1) thinking ahead,

(2) weighing the evidence, (3) summarizing what has been said, and (4) listening between the lines. In the give-and-take of a conference there is plenty of time for the conferees to exercise these four mental processes upon the line of thought being pursued by the group as a whole. The following four questions give an idea of how each process might be made to function when a person listens at a conference.

1. Is the group's line of thought leading us toward, or taking us away from, the solution of the problem at hand?
2. Is the evidence being presented by the person speaking pertinent to the topic we are pursuing?
3. What have we as a group accomplished so far toward the solution of the problem under discussion?
4. Are we functioning as a group, or are certain individuals in the group skirting some area that should be talked about?

These four thought processes, when used in listening to an individual, help keep the listener from going off on mental sidetracks that cause him to lose the pursued line of thought. When used by conferees on a group's line of spoken thought, the four processes help keep the entire discussion on the track most effective for it to take. These mental ingredients of aural concentration help each conferee to discover what the common problem is, and they guide him in making oral contributions that relate to the emerging course of action designed to solve the problem.

TUNE IN—TUNE OUT

Another conference stumbling block is caused by what we have called "emotional filters." They affect all of us when we listen. In general, as you recall, the filters cause us to shut out what we don't want to hear and carefully assimilate what we do want to hear. You can safely assume that in any conference, emotional filters are at work all around the table.

At a meeting of people, let us say that a man named Hornsby is a participant. Like all the others at the meeting, Hornsby has his own private point of view on the problem at hand, a position built out of his special interests and experiences. He gladly presents it to the meeting and assumes that all his fellow participants understand and accept what he has to say. But on the other side of the table another conferee starts presenting his viewpoint, and it happens to be quite different from Hornsby's. If Hornsby does what he assumed the conferees did when he talked, he will listen very carefully to the other fellow's statement, trying to decide whether or not it is better than his own. But listening at conferences seldom follows such a pattern, because emotional filters go to work. Before the other fellow has spoken very much Hornsby "mentally tunes out" what is coming into his ears. He doesn't care to hear something that will cast doubt upon the validity of his own position. So Hornsby, instead of listening, figures out what he can say at the first opportunity to "make those fools across the table" understand the "good solid outlook" he has on the problem.

Hornsby's type of listening is diametrically opposed to the basic concept of what makes a successful conference. A meeting of people fulfills its problem-solving function only when the participants give *all* their different viewpoints a fair hearing, and then select the best of what has been presented for use in solving the problem at hand. When individuals filter out the statements that don't match their private outlooks, the conference as a whole is weakened. The old saw of "two heads are better than one" no longer works, because the two heads are working independently of each other.

If, at the beginning of a meeting, the conference leader will take a moment to point out that the participants may be affected by emotional filters, then the filters may not cause as much difficulty as they might otherwise. The leader can also fight the influence of the filters by setting a norm for the meeting: that the conference should be considered a place where each participant can speak his mind and expect all the other people to hear him out.

In an earlier chapter two aids to hearing people out were cited: (1) withholding evaluation, and (2) hunting for negative evidence.

Here is an important way in which "withholding evaluation" helps conference participants:

In conferences a talker often starts what he has to say with a sweeping generalization. In the spontaneous give-and-take of a meeting, a generalization is not always carefully thought out and may not faithfully represent what the speaker really means. Such a generalization, however, often contains the words and phrases that trigger off a listener's emotional filters. Listening stops and the speaker's real meaning, as outlined in the evidence that he gives following the generalization, may not be heard.

At an industrial conference the head of the estimating department says, "I've been having a rough time lately getting cooperation out of some people when I need cost figures."

He goes on to amplify this generalization, but people around the table, an accountant, an engineer and a plant superintendent, are shutting out the words that follow. They don't consider themselves uncooperative and they resent such a statement. Instead of listening they mentally prepare rebuttals.

185

Meanwhile the estimating department head goes on to explain that "it took two weeks to get an answer to a query back from the research division."

Though his generalization seemed broad, the man was really concerned about only one small area of the whole plant, the research division. But those who shut him off never learn this fact, and they plunge into the meeting with all kinds of defensive statements that take the conference off on a number of tangents.

The second aid to hearing people out—"hunting for negative evidence"—concerns how human beings treat the business of similarities and differences. In general we look for things that are similar to what we know and fail to see things that are different. In the oral discourse of a conference where many people meet, there are likely to be more differences than similarities. A listener, if he is to be a worthwhile participant, must make a special effort to hear the differences. To his ears they often sound like negative evidence, for they don't agree with what he thinks. But in searching for the differences, the listener is making an effort to overcome prejudices produced by his emotional filters.

THE DECISIONS GET BETTER

When people at a conference make the effort to hear each other out they are likely to bring their private worlds closer to the actual world, and the group's decisions are almost certain to be more valid. A partner of Management Development Associates in New York, J. Collins Coffee, illustrates this premise for executive seminars by drawing a large "X" on a blackboard. One line of the "X" represents the "real" world and the other line represents an individual's private world built upon experience obtained in only a narrow segment of the "real" world.

"You can see," says Coffee, "that these two lines could work at cross purposes with one another if we base our decision making only upon the line built by individual experience. The decisions are not likely to gibe very closely with the state of things in the real world.

"On the other hand, our decision making will be more valid if we also draw more from the real world around us. Careful listening to other people's ideas, viewpoints and experiences is the best way I know of doing this. When you listen to another person you, in effect, get one more view, or slice, of what the real world is like. The more you listen to the different points of view that different people present on a matter, the more accurate becomes the picture of the way things *actually* may be concerning that matter."

The business of hearing people out also offers a conference some interesting by-products.

LISTEN TO HIM TALK, TALK, TALK

First, it may serve as a means of handling participants who continually pop up with objections or verbal contributions that have nothing to do with the task at hand. Trying to subdue such people by talking them down often produces the opposite results; they come back all the harder, fighting to inject their objections or ideas. Far less time is wasted when the members of a conference take the opposite tack with such people and "listen them out."

The New York Adult Education Council held a "listening clinic" which operated like a conference to discuss the problem of bad listening. Among those attending was a middle-aged matron who frequently blocked the clinic's progress by talking incessantly on all sorts of subjects. She soon became a serious problem, and her fellow participants in the clinic discussed privately how they should handle the woman. "We're talking about listening," said one of the people. "Why don't we try it out on her? Tonight, let's allow her to talk and we'll really listen to her."

The lady came into the clinic and soon she was off on her verbal spree. Everyone turned to her and paid very close attention to all she had to say. The woman didn't talk long; suddenly she stopped, looked very puzzled and blurted out, "Why, everybody is listening to me!" After that the clinic proceeded with a greatly reduced number of interruptions from the lady.

FOSTERING CREATIVITY

The second by-product of hearing people out at a conference has to do with creativity. The freedom to talk to people who will listen without interrupting has the effect of cultivating creativity. When a person feels free to express himself, ideas that have been lying dormant deep inside him sometimes come to mind and he speaks them.

The principle of "brainstorming" is based upon this same premise. In brainstorming sessions a hard and fast rule is laid down: "Under no circumstances shall participants interrupt to judge ideas that are being voiced!" Few people will deny that brainstorming sessions produce plenty of ideas. In fact the critics of this form of creativity say that it produces almost too many ideas, and the task of selecting the best ones becomes the stumbling block in the process.

However, as a by-product of good listening habits in a conference, the cultivation of creativity should lead in a positive direction most of the time.

There is one more phase of listening, the ability to analyze oral persuasion, that plays an important part in a conference.

As Richard Beckhard of Conference Counselors points out, people arrive at a meeting with strong urges to influence their fellow conferees. Often the urge to influence people is turned into action by a conferee using the oral persuasion techniques discussed earlier in the book. If his listeners do not exercise their critical abilities upon what he says, the persuasive participant may actually make the conference's decisions by himself.

Critical listening, as stated before, means testing what the talker has to say. It does not mean jumping to conclusions by making final judgments before a person finishes speaking.

When any person speaks in a conference, the things he says should be tested by the people around him. Does his evidence fully support the proposals he states? How old is his evidence, and does its age affect it in any way? What is the source of the talker's evidence, and how competent is it? Is he strongly prejudiced in some way for what he proposes, or is he likely to be neutral about it? Through such questions as these the listener weighs what each participant contributes to the group's thinking.

When conferees exercise critical listening they are not so likely to be unduly influenced by a single member of the group. On the other hand, if the contributions of a single member are the most worthwhile ones, then critical listening will help assure that his contributions are used properly.

Perhaps now the important part played by listening in group discussions is more obvious. Yet its significance is not always understood by people in conferences. Too often they feel that participation occurs only while an individual is talking. Measured as a part of the whole conference process, talking becomes only a small part of group participation. Listening, however, when widely used by conferees, greatly enlarges the total amount of participation of each person in the group. Dr. Arthur Kellner, a New York industrial psychologist, explains how the amount of participation is important to decision making.

"In the decision-making situation," he states, "the degree of acceptance of the group decision by any individual depends upon the extent to which he participated in the process. This relationship is geometric rather than arithmetic—that is, twice as much participation might result in four times as much identification with the decision."

Sidney Stricker, president of the I. W. Harper–Ancient Age Distillers Company, tells of a young New York advertising executive who went to Kentucky and held a conference with a group of whisky distributors. The eager young man grasped the initiative at the meeting and talked for over an hour without allowing anyone else to speak. He finished by asking, "Well, what have you boys got to say?"

There was a silence, so he turned to the head distributor, a huge, easy-going Kentuckian, and said, "Well, hasn't anybody got anything to contribute here?"

"No, sir," was the answer, "*you* said it all!"

190

Here are seven specific suggestions designed to help improve conference listening. Some are especially valuable to conference leaders; the others will be most valuable to training directors.

1. Plan conferences as far ahead as possible. For each conference write a statement of its purpose and distribute copies to each conferee, asking him to prepare to contribute all the facts and ideas that he can in regard to the central problem that will be discussed. If possible at the meeting itself, set a deadline for making recommendations or reaching a decision. When these steps are taken, people are better motivated for listening during the discussion.

2. In a training session, plan and hold a conference on a selected problem as described above, and tape-record it. Afterward, play back the recording. Discuss it in terms of listening. Do the contributions of different participants reflect good listening? If the conference goes off track, try to analyze the causes.

3. In a training session, assign one problem to two groups. Ask them to meet in separate rooms and reach their decisions within a time limit. Record both discussions. Bring the groups together and play back the recordings. Compare the decisions made by the two groups. Which group seemed to do the better listening? How was that group's listening reflected in its decision?

4. Get permission to record an actual conference. Play back the recording before a training group. Ask the conferees to apply the four listening concentration skills dis-

cussed in this chapter. Part way through the recording, turn it off and ask the trainees to write: (1) summaries of what they have heard, (2) predictions of the conference's outcome and (3) a short commentary on the evidence they heard presented. Allow the trainees to hear the remaining part of the recorded conference, and hold a discussion of the entire exercise.

5. When acting as a conference leader with a group meeting for the first time, give a one-minute talk emphasizing the importance of listening. Ask all to agree that they will make an effort to hear each other out.

6. At the start of a meeting use the formula discussed early in this chapter to determine how much more listening than talking will be required during the session. For the answer subtract one from the total number of conferees. Print the answer on a card placed in the center of the table. The number represents how many people should be listening when one person is speaking.

7. After a conference, if time allows, hold a listening critique. Ask each conference member to evaluate the listening attention that he received while talking, and to report an analysis of his own listening performance.

Chapter 15

The Family Listening Circle

The coherence of a family group depends to a large degree upon communication through the spoken word. The family members talk and listen to one another. The "talking" phase of family communication ordinarily takes care of itself, but the "listening" phase frequently gives rise to numerous problems.

People from homes with strong family ties can often recall that someone in the house placed emphasis on the need for listening. A colleague of mine remembers what happened during the evening meal in his family.

"At home," he says, "dinner began promptly at six o'clock. After taking our places at the table, Father would invariably ask my youngest brother, Jim, to tell us what he had been doing or thinking about that day. As my brother talked we were encouraged to listen, and to take an active interest in what he said. Somehow Father made it subconsciously understood that while Jim talked the time was his, and we were not to interrupt unless we had something pertinent to add to what he had to say.

"Next Father let my young sister know that it was her

turn to talk, and when she had finished it became my turn. I was the oldest child.

"This taking of turns was not forced upon us in a stern, disciplinary fashion. Frequently the procedure broke up into a free-for-all discussion. But no matter what happened, Father acted as a friendly moderator and insisted that we listen courteously to one another. We learned that we could talk freely about anything, any problems, any ideas. Some of the ideas that we voiced seem fantastic now, but they were never squelched."

If there is any one place in the world that we should be free to speak our minds, it's at home within our family group. The foundation of this freedom is listening, and in return for the freedom each family member must help lay the foundation by doing his share as a listener.

CHILDREN NEED TO BE HEARD TOO

Perhaps above all, the family should be attentive to the very youngest child. As a toddler begins to talk, when his thinking is still largely in the realm of fantasy, he is urgently in need of the listening which can be furnished by parents and older brothers and sisters.

"The child should be stimulated to express his fantasies to the trusted parents," says Margaret A. Ribble, well-known child psychiatrist. "These fantasies are usually startling to the adult, but the very expression of them helps the child correct the unreality of some of his first thinking."

To stimulate the child's self-expression is an important listening function for the elders in his family. If a child is encouraged to talk freely with an adult listener, he will find an important contact with the world around him, the world of grown-ups, of reality. Without the listener a child turns elsewhere to seek an avenue leading to the reality that he needs. If a child has no listeners, he may resort to the mass media of radio and television as an avenue to reality, and sometimes what he finds there doesn't serve as the best of introductions to the grown-up's world.

As the youngster moves toward adolescence he continues to need adult listeners. Slowly he comes more and more into contact with the world outside his home and faces new notions and problems that need clarification. The child can't always talk freely among his friends, so he returns home for someone to talk to. In his home the youngster must find at least one sympathetic, understanding listener among his elders. The listener must be a person who will make every effort to hear the young one out, who won't chop off conversations with such statements as: "Don't bother me with that!" or "That's another crazy notion you've picked up; forget it!" The listener must have the patience that goes with hearing a boy or girl talk about the same things over and over again. This listener should understand that he is witnessing an amazing phenomenon, that of a human being developing, feeling his way in the realm of ideas, in search of those that can help build a personal philosophy.

Without the freedom of talking to a good listener, the developing child's problems remain, and often grow, within the youngster. Then the child's thoughts may find less desirable outlets—sometimes through what we call "juvenile delinquency." As a result the parents may be forced to listen to the child's thoughts, but perhaps too late, for the words may come through a school official, the police or a court.

AURAL IMITATION

While good parental listening provides a youngster with needed guidance as he develops, it also serves a dual purpose; for *how* the parents listen to a child has a bearing on how the child will listen to other people.

Listening is an act that can be imitated, just as talking, walking or anything else that a young one learns. When parents are good listeners their offspring are likely to be the same. In questioning college students in regard to their home life I have discovered that the better listeners usually come from families in which the parents seemed to be thoughtful listeners. The worst listener encountered in my experience as a teacher was a product of a mother who talked and apparently never listened. The boy was mentioned earlier in the book, and you may recall that as a result of his mother's never-ending harangues he taught himself to "just reach up and turn off" everyone who spoke any length of time to him.

AND THE GROWN-UPS TOO

The need for listeners at home is not only centered upon children. Adults also need to be heard by one another. In many instances the only possible listener we have recourse to is a husband or wife. If one's spouse is not a sympathetic listener, one is often left alone with thoughts that can boil up inside until there is trouble. With a good listener troublesome thoughts can sometimes be "talked out" into nothingness.

In the human structuring of today's business world a man often finds that he cannot discuss all of his problems, ideas or fears at his place of work, and that if he holds them inside for too long, they produce undue stress that becomes unbearable. Many times a wife is the only person in the world to whom many of a man's most important thoughts can be voiced. The very act of the husband's talking to his wife—if she is a sympathetic listener—will sometimes alleviate pressure created by the thoughts within him.

On the other hand, a wife who spends her days alone or with only young children needs a listener. Again, hers is a case of problems, ideas and fears building up inside with no adult outlet through which they can be released. A husband who listens with understanding may often relieve the stress that develops during the wife's day at home.

When poor listening exists between a husband and wife, one or the other, or both, may take the same action that a child does when no one at home will hear what he has to say. In their need for listeners they may turn away from home to receive satisfaction.

The husband may spend his time giving vent to his thoughts to a bartender. Or he may find another woman, one who listens to him.

The wife may spend her days phoning one friend after another, seeking someone who listens well. Or through the medium of gossip she may feel that she can unburden herself orally. Or she may also turn from the husband to another man, one who listens to her.

DEVELOPING AURAL EXPERIENCES

While attention to family listening is important in the routine course of events, the members should also plan listening experiences that can be shared by everyone at one time.

The term "family listening circle" comes to my mind because of what happened at home when I was a child. My mother liked to read, and she wanted her children to take an interest in reading. She had an excellent way of creating this interest.

Nearly every evening we would sit on the floor around

her in the living room, and she would read aloud to us for an hour or so. Frequently the neighbors' children came to join our family listening circle and together we heard the great stories that I now associate with childhood. As we grew older she adjusted to our development by selecting things to read that met our growing mental abilities. For example, she would sometimes read an editorial from the daily newspaper or a current magazine article, and afterward we would spend a few minutes talking about what we had heard.

In recent years, out of curiosity, I have made an informal survey among friends by asking two questions: Do you read a lot? Did either of your parents read aloud to you when you were a youngster? More often than not, when the answer to the first question is "Yes," the answer to the second question will be the same.

A management engineer from Hurley, New York, C. L. Christensen, was asked these two questions. It turned out that his mother had made oral reading an evening custom, and it had instilled in her son a desire to read.

"By the time I reached the fourth grade of our one-room school," said Christensen, "I had read every volume in the school library. There were only forty-eight books, but by reading them I set a record for the school."

Oral reading is an activity that any family can cultivate without difficulty. Reading aloud to children can help them in at least two ways: (1) It improves their listening ability, which is an asset in school and in life, and (2) it develops an interest in books that serves as a valuable motivating force for silent reading.

And, of course, listening to someone read stories is a deep source of pleasure to most youngsters.

An industrial plant at Gallatin, Tennessee, has a free lending library for employees who wish to take books home for reading aloud to their children. The library became popular immediately after it was installed. A while after it was started, a questionnaire was sent to employees asking them about the oral reading program. Over half the parents answering the questionnaires mentioned occasions when children turned to the oral reading rather than a favorite radio or television program. The answered questionnaires indicated that most people would also like to borrow books that could be read aloud to teenagers and adults.

RADIO AND TV NEED SELECTIVITY

In my opinion the family listening circle now has more reason for existing than ever before. Radio and television present an excellent opportunity for sharing listening experiences that are helpful to children. With the mass media especially, children need occasional guidance in selecting the programs to which they listen. Now and then adults should join children in listening to programs other than the routine comedy shows, quiz programs and serialized dramas. There are excellent documentary programs, panel discussions, drama, news and special education features that provide listening experiences. The value of such programs can be enhanced by discussing them with children after they have been heard.

If the budget allows, the family can profit from a library of spoken-word phonograph recordings. They can provide pleasure for everyone, plus helpful listening experiences for children. Spoken-word records, available through most record dealers, offer prose, poetry and drama of the best quality, including selections made especially for children. As explained earlier in the book, on many of these records you hear authors reading aloud from their own writings.

Record companies are also selling recordings of famous speeches. And there are records like the *Hear It Now* series which allow listeners to hear history as it was made.

Again if the budget allows, a tape recorder can contribute to a family's listening activities. Radio and television programs that have listening value can be caught, preserved and heard over and over again. Children like to record their own "radio" plays and listen to them later. If a family in another town has a tape recorder too, their children can communicate with yours by tape rather than letter. One family makes a recording addressed to the other family. The tape is mailed the same as a letter. The family receiving it listens to the message, records an answer and mails the tape back. Everyone, from the youngest child to the father and mother, can speak his piece on a "tape letter."

Another aural experience that can be shared by a family is the listening game. "Twenty Questions" is one example, and if you're interested in others there are a number of listening games described at the end of Chapter 16.

THE EAR NEEDS EXPERIENCE

In any of these home activities where children are involved there is a principle that parents should observe if they wish to develop the youngster's listening ability. It is this: The parents should make conscious attempts to upgrade the children's aural experiences as time passes.

When a child's listening activities are allowed to develop without occasional guidance, they are almost certain to gravitate toward easier and easier listening. As a result, the child does not gain experience at listening to things that require much mental exertion. At some point in his life this lack of listening experience can be a serious handicap. For instance, it may be his downfall in college where suddenly he finds that a great deal of learning must come through listening to lectures which require considerable mental exertion.

To upgrade a child's listening the parents should regularly join the child in hearing something that may be just a bit beyond his ability to understand aurally. It would help if on such occasions the parents could let the child know that listening sometimes, like sports, can be a challenge. It takes effort now and then to improve, but when the challenge is met, the aural experience that results becomes a most satisfying one.

TALKING THINGS OVER AND LISTENING

In many homes today family members set aside a special period for talking and listening to one another. The meetings may occur around the dinner table, as was the case in the home of my colleague mentioned earlier. Or the meetings may be held in the living room at a particular time. Everyone gathers around and the entire group discusses anything and everything pertinent to the family. Problems are ironed out; common experiences are recalled and discussed; stories and anecdotes are told; and family plans are made.

Such meetings are delightful in many ways. And once listening is established as a necessary ingredient—perhaps through the moderating abilities of a father or mother—the get-togethers take on new and important meaning.

Family members learn to listen to differences of opinion. This, as we've mentioned several times in previous chapters, is not an easy thing to do. But to "hear people out" without getting entangled in what they are saying is an ability that can be valuable to a person throughout his life.

The development of this ability "to hear people out" has a valuable by-product, especially for the children at the family meeting. When they are listened to, they feel free to express all kinds of ideas. This freedom of expression leaves children unafraid to talk to people when talking is the thing to do.

The family meeting that places emphasis upon listening also develops a sense of aural responsibility in children. They learn how important it is to understand each other through the spoken word, and that to obtain the understanding, at least half of the success depends upon someone's listening. This concept, when understood by children, leads to listening manners which are as important as speaking manners, table manners or party manners.

In conclusion, I might say that almost anything that an entire family can do as a group stands to improve the members' ability to listen. A family trip to the zoo, a ride in the automobile, going to a movie as a group, taking in a lecture, going shopping together, building something as a group—anything where everybody is included is likely to help in respect to listening. The reason is fairly simple: When people do things together they have something of common interest to talk about. With talk that has common interest, people are motivated to listen and they gain experience at the skill.

When emphasis is placed on hearing and understanding one another at home, words that are spoken give strength to family ties that can last forever.

Chapter 16

Listening at School

A colleague of mine was at a dinner party in New York City a while ago and a lady heard him say that he was interested in listening education.

"Listening?" asked the lady. "What do you mean by that?"

"Well, what you're doing right this second," explained the man. "We're interested in teaching students how to listen."

"But how can you teach listening?" said the lady. "There's nothing that you can see to study. You can't see sound waves!"

Such queries are not unusual in our visually oriented society. The factors involved in aural assimilation seem too abstruse to be organized and used for classroom purposes. Listening is something you either do or don't do, we hear people say. A course in it seems no more feasible than a course in breathing or walking. We are continually asked, "What do you do to teach listening?"

The answer to this question is twofold. When teaching students to listen we first motivate them by increasing their awareness of the values obtainable through the auditory channels of learning; then we build experience in the habits that make for effective listening.

People who have a compelling reason to listen well and who practice the skill will often hear and understand things that most of us miss.

Telephone operators, for instance, often become acute listeners.

A few years ago in Streetman, Texas, an excited farmer rang the local telephone operator to tell her that a car driven by two men had just run off the road near his home. He had gone for a team to pull the auto out of the ditch, but when he returned, the two men had disappeared. Looking around the area, he stumbled across a Missouri license plate and a couple of guns hidden in the brush nearby.

"What'll I do?" the farmer asked the operator.

"Tell me what the men looked like," she said. After the farmer had described the two men, the operator rang the sheriff's office. Before going on duty, she told the law officer, she had heard a news broadcast. Six Springfield, Missouri, police officers had been shot to death. The broadcast had described the killers, the operator said, and the description fitted the two men who had ditched the car in Streetman.

Following the telephone operator's tip, police caught up with the two fugitives in Houston, Texas, and surrounded them. Rather than submit to capture, the men killed themselves. And when police inspected the bodies, they found that the telephone operator had been right; the two men were indeed the killers.

Chances are that most of us wouldn't have remembered the description even if we had heard the radio broadcast, because we lack the listening motivation and experience of the telephone operator.

The poorest listeners of all, we have found, are inexperienced at listening to difficult, expository material. On the other hand, our best listeners find ways of obtaining such experience.

This fact is supported by a study that I completed at the University of Minnesota a few years ago. Several hundred freshmen were tested for listening ability. The one hundred best and the one hundred poorest listeners were carefully studied through personal interviews, written questionnaires and several kinds of objective tests. Among other questions, the students were asked about their radio listening.

Of the poorest listeners, fewer than 5 per cent listened to programs requiring concentrated aural attention, programs comparable to *Meet the Press, America's Town Meeting of the Air, The Chicago Round Table* and *American Forum of the Air.* As a matter of fact, many of the students indicated that they were not even acquainted with the titles of these presentations.

The one hundred best listeners told of listening frequently to this type of radio program. A large number of the one hundred expressed a definite liking for several of these educational or semi-educational offerings.

The same kind of contrast resulted between the two groups when they were asked about attending educational lectures in their home communities. The poorer listeners hardly ever went to lectures, while the better listeners frequently attended.

Why do we find such widespread inexperience at listening to difficult material among college freshmen? The answer is partially given by the fact that, in terms of training, the eye has been the "favored son" of educators, whereas the ear has been the "neglected child."

But there's more to the problem than neglect of training. Perhaps more serious is the fact that poor listening is frequently accepted as a necessary evil.

Mrs. Philip Richards, a schoolteacher in Midland, Michigan, has summed up what happens when we tolerate slipshod aural habits.

"In school," she says, "from the child's advent into kindergarten until his graduation from high school, the present educational setup does the best it can to discourage the use of ears. The instructor, anxious to give the child a good start, repeats information and directions so many times that the child learns to expect such reiteration. Why listen the first time when he can get it on the sixth or seventh round?"

Mrs. Richards goes on to tell how directions for school procedure are repeated and repeated over public-address systems. The students are not held responsible for listening and comprehending the message when it is stated the first time. Often a mimeographed version of the message is distributed as a final step in communication.

"The student's very soul," says Mrs. Richards, "depends on a good mimeograph." Lecturers accompany their talks with mimeographed outlines to assist the poor listeners. Tests and test instructions that could be given orally are cranked out on the mimeograph machine. Messages to parents are not entrusted to oral communication through the pupils.

The schools are not alone guilty for supporting the half-listener. For instance, radio announcements are often repeated and simplified until only the feeblest mental effort is required for comprehension. Television announcements are often given in both spoken and printed words, which are again repeated and simplified.

Most teachers today are more than willing to admit that the improvement of listening is something that is very much desired in our schools, but while they recognize this need they are often stumped by the apparent problems which must be solved to fulfill the need. First comes the problem of time. The curriculums in most of today's schools are already overloaded with subjects. To add another subject often seems impossible to the overworked teacher. And, secondly, many a teacher is stopped for lack of the know-how needed to teach listening. She is unable to find textbooks on the subject, and course outlines for different grades of school are largely nonexistent.

The problem of time is a real one, but possibly not as serious as often thought to be. In the first place, much can be done to improve listening ability without sandwiching new courses into an already tight curriculum. Listening improvement can come by integrating it with currently established classroom activities of an oral nature. This way of getting at the subject is presently at work in a number of schools.

GOOD LISTENING PAYS FOR ITSELF

But let's say that a teacher decides to squeeze a separate unit of listening instruction into her busy curriculum.

Will it be a good investment? I feel that such training will continue to pay dividends for many years. With improved listening comes a learning economy that is valuable throughout school and life. Less oral repetition is needed by teachers. When appropriate, they can depend more upon lectures, which means that a single person talking can teach a great number of students at one time. And there's even an important by-product to improved aural assimilation. Effective listeners are almost certain to produce fewer disciplinary problems.

The next question, how to do it, is not so easily solved. Instructional material for listening improvement usually has to be created by the teacher herself. Slowly, it is safe to predict, prepared listening courses will be developed and made available to teachers. Already the professional journals, especially in speech and English, are printing a number of articles outlining procedures for teaching listening. And there are a few textbooks, mostly in the field of speech education, that have chapters or sections on listening. But even without the help of prepared material, the development of listening-improvement procedures need not be too difficult a task for a teacher.

The Nashville, Tennessee, public schools present us with a good example of what can be done in this field of learning. A few years ago, the schools' English Steering Committee made a survey of the pupils' listening abilities. Tests were developed to see how well the youngsters could do such things as "get the main idea" and "draw inferences or conclusions" from what they heard. A total of 8,316 pupils from grades one to twelve were tested. Two hundred and thirty teachers in 45 schools participated in the Nashville survey. From the results, the Steering Committee saw a need to look into the problem of listening, and further work on the subject was recommended.

The recommendation was followed up with more studies from which were developed procedures for teaching listening. The studies following the original survey were integrated with normal classroom and school activities. The report on listening from the Nashville work states: "There are so many regular day-by-day situations in which good listening techniques can be developed that teachers who are sensitive to the need and awake to the opportunities do not need extra activities designed solely as exercises in listening." Eventually manuals were written for grades one through twelve to help teachers improve their pupils' listening ability.

THREE ATTACKS

Drawing from what has already been done in other institutions and from my own work at the University of Minnesota, I feel there are three approaches to listening improvement feasible for use in our schools. Depending upon current curriculum arrangements and the availability of personnel to carry through with these approaches, any combination of them might be put to work.

1. The direct approach

This approach depends upon setting aside classroom time for specific courses in listening. It involves several activities. First, through lectures a case for good listening is built in order to give students an understanding of *why* they will profit from efforts to improve their aural abilities. Such lectures are accompanied by group discussions of listening as a medium of learning. Next come classroom discussions of listening skills. As they are introduced, the pupils are given exercises to develop the skills. Special consideration is given to listening concentration by frequently exposing pupils to oral material that, because of its degree of difficulty, requires a real expenditure of effort to understand. The difficulty of such oral material is progressively increased as the pupils improve. Periodic progress tests are given to measure such factors as comprehension, ability to get main ideas and critical ability. And the over-all influence of the aural training course is verified by before-and-after measurements based upon standardized tests of this skill.*

2. The integrated approach

For schools that cannot give separate courses labeled "Listening" because of tightly packed curriculums, lack of personnel or other problems, this approach may be a solution. It requires coordination of listening instruction with other subjects—especially those concerned with the language arts. A school wishing to take this approach might start by selecting a committee of teachers to study and recommend ways of integrating listening with current courses of study. Among its other purposes, the committee would have the task of helping all of the school's staff to become aware of (1) how improved listening might benefit teachers and students, and (2) how teachers might develop listening activities to fit into their present syllabi. The committee would seek ways of building listening responsibility in students on a school-wide basis by the use of assembly programs and announcements made through

* The Educational Testing Service, Princeton, N.J., has completed a listening test for the lower grades. This will supplement those measures already standardized and commercially available for more adult grades.

public-address systems. And the committee would assist teachers to design tests measuring listening improvement.

3. *The listening laboratory*

This method of listening improvement does not preclude the use of the above two approaches, but supplements them. The listening laboratory would include the following features:

+ A partially soundproofed room, acoustically treated if possible. The room, if budget allows, would have acoustically treated cubicles for individual use.

+ A library of spoken-word recordings (tape, disk, or both) and playback equipment. The recordings would include as many commercial spoken-word records as the budget permits: authors reading their writings, actors reading classical literature, famous speeches, instructional-type recordings on a variety of subjects, children's stories, drama and the *Hear It Now* type of recordings. The library might also include disks or tapes made by teachers, guest speakers, student drama groups, etc.—assuming, of course, that the school has recording equipment.

+ A radio, and possibly a television set, for "controlled use" limited to programs selected by teachers for educational purposes.

+ Objective tests constructed by the teachers to cover at least a portion of the recorded material, especially the instructional records.

+ Indexing and filing of the recorded material according to its difficulty.

eduled times the laboratory should be available
nts who care to listen to spoken-word records for
, or instructional records for academic reasons.
such hours a competent attendant should be on
operate the equipment. For the remainder of the
time, the laboratory would be available to teachers. They
could use it in conjunction with listening-improvement
activities and to supplement other classroom studies.
Teachers, for instance, might make assignments requiring
students to use the laboratory as they now use a library of
books.

After selection of an approach to listening instruction
in a school, a little imagination and ingenuity on the part
of the staff will certainly produce a program that will go
a long way toward correcting current deficiencies. Pupils
will be receiving a new kind of aural experience, and an
extremely helpful one.

FORTY–FOUR THINGS TO DO

It is beyond this chapter's scope to spell out courses of
listening instruction that might be used at different school
grade levels. However, immediately following are forty-
four suggestions for use in classrooms. The list has been
drawn from the work done at such schools as those at
Nashville, Phoenix, Cincinnati, and Minneapolis; from
college listening courses; from educational journals and
from my own thinking. A few of these suggestions may be
applied in any classroom from grade one through twelve.
In general, however, lower-grade teachers might draw
mainly from the first third of the suggestions, intermediate
grade teachers from the second third, and high-school
teachers from the final third. No attempt has been made at
recommending tests to go with the suggestions, but upon

212

reading the list a teacher will surely recognize opportunities for testing different factors of listening comprehension.

1. As a teacher, inventory your own listening and talking. If you talk very much more than you listen to the pupils, try to bring the situation into closer balance. Children imitate listening as well as anything else they observe.

2. Try to present orally many of the regular tests in all subjects. Read a test's instructions aloud, and also all of the questions, giving the pupils time to write each answer.

3. When there are messages to be carried by pupils from classroom to classroom, or classroom to home, try putting the communication on an oral basis.

4. Ask the children to list all of the sounds they hear in a given period of time; for instance, a bird singing outside the window, the noise of an airplane passing overhead, the teacher's voice, etc. Discuss what sounds the children like or dislike and why. Also discuss what sounds are most important and why.

5. Speak the last syllable of a word to the class ("ick," for example). Ask the pupils to speak aloud as many words as possible ending in the same sound (like tick, sick, pick, etc.) without repeating any words.

6. Read the description of a physical scene to the class. Encourage the youngsters to draw pictures from what they heard.

7. Read aloud a poem which is likely to evoke emotion, and then encourage the pupils to discuss their feelings.

8. After hearing a song, ask the children to describe the story behind the song's words.

9. Whisper a short message to a child at one side of the classroom. Ask him to relay the material, in a whisper, to the child nearest him. Continue this procedure until the message has been passed to every child around the room. Ask the last child to repeat aloud what he heard, and then compare it with the original paragraph whispered to the first child. Try this game frequently in an effort to make the relayed message match the original as closely as possible.

10. Play a listening game by giving increasingly difficult instructions to one child and then another. To the first child you might say: "Peter, take the apple from the desk and place it on the chair." To the next child: "Fred, take the apple from the chair, show it to Mary and then return it to the desk." To the next child: "Ellen, take the apple from the desk, show it to Peter, show it to Fred and then put it on the chair." The game of instructions continues until someone fails to follow the directions correctly.

11. Play a listening game which asks that each child in turn repeat the words he has just heard and add one more word. The teacher gives the first word, such as "The," and calls on a pupil to add a word. He may say, "The house . . ." The next child might say, "The house that . . ." The game continues until a participant fails to repeat the words correctly or to add a word that makes sense.

12. In all class activities, make a policy of not repeating instructions. If repetition is necessary, call on the pupils to repeat what was stated. Establish the same policy in regard to the school public-address system, that announcements will be made only once and repetitions will have to come from classmates.

13. Encourage the children to develop a set of standards for good listening; print and post them in the classroom. The standards should be decided upon through class discussion. One such standard might be: "The good listener keeps his eyes on the person talking."

14. Read a short poem to the class and ask the pupils to guess the title, or to make up a title. Encourage the children to give reasons for their choices.

15. When children are absent from class, give those present the assignment of summarizing and passing on orally the instructions missed by the absentees.

16. Select a few paragraphs of narrative material from a book or story and read aloud. Have members of the class act out what they heard.

17. When a guest speaker is coming to the school, have a discussion with the children concerning what the person might talk about. After the speech have another discussion concerning what the speaker did talk about. Try to direct the second discussion toward determining the speaker's main point.

18. Occasionally play the game of "Twenty Questions." Build the game around people or things currently being considered in classroom studies, such as history or literature.

19. Develop a class discussion on listening manners. For example, a discussion might evolve around the question: "Why is it important to 'hear out' what a person has to say?"

20. From a play or story select a few hundred words of pure conversation between two or more characters. Read it aloud to the class and then have the pupils guess the story behind the conversation.

21. Read descriptions of well-known people—perhaps people being studied in class—and have the students guess their names.

22. Give the class a brief, simple description of what nonverbal communication means (see Chapter 5). Then ask different students to speak two or three words, giving them different meanings by varying their voices, using gestures, etc. For example, you might use the sentence, "I want you." One child might say it with a snarl. Another might say it in soft, gentle tones. Another might snap it out abruptly. Ask the class to give the different meanings the phrase acquires with each utterance.

23. Explain to the class that what we hear is often affected by senses other than hearing. For each of these senses discuss how it might affect listening. For example, with the sense of touch, the discussion might develop around how the feeling of a handshake affects what we hear.

24. Ask the pupils, in pairs, to interview each other on hobbies or special interests. After the interviews talk about the possibilities of learning by this method. Discuss the advantages and disadvantages of interviewing as compared to reading.

25. Ask three or four students to prepare short talks on a favorite subject. Tell the student speakers that they may have to talk under very difficult circumstances that are being planned, but no matter what happens they should continue speaking and not take personal offense.

Ask them to leave the room. Instruct the class to listen very carefully to what each speaker says, until the class receives a secret signal from you. At the signal the students are to stop paying attention, perhaps to start to read books or to look out the window. Call the student speakers into the room, one at a time, and ask them to give their talks. When they are finished, ask the speakers to discuss how they felt when the class withdrew its attention. Follow this with a class discussion about the listener's responsibility to the speaker (see Chapter 3).

26. Select written material that contains words unfamilar to the students and list the words on the blackboard. Read the material aloud after asking the students to seek out the words' meanings from the context of what is heard.

27. Read a story or play and ask the class to plan a good stage setting for acting out what was heard.

28. Explain the précis method of taking notes (see Chapter 10). Select a short speech containing several points. Read the speech, stopping for about thirty seconds after each completed point. During this pause the students should write a one-or-two sentence précis of what they have heard. Ask them to number each précis to correspond with each pause. Collect the notes; prepare an oral critique of them to be presented to the class.

29. Ask the students to make a list of what they like very much to hear and what they dislike hearing. Develop a discussion around the list. Look for personal reasons that make some material easy listening and other material difficult listening (see Chapter 8).

30. Conduct a class discussion on a subject of current interest to the students. Make a tape recording of all the

conversations. Play back the recording and then ask the students to discuss the oral composition of what they heard. Is it different from the way things are written in books? Are these differences significant to the skill of listening? (See Chapter 5.)

31. Compose a short, argumentative talk on a subject that is of concern to the students. Among the ideas that strengthen the argument, include a few ideas that have little to do with the subject. Ask the students, as they hear the talk, to try separating the essential and nonessential ideas. Discuss the project afterward.

32. Ask the class members to write down all the words they can that affect them emotionally (see Chapter 8). Compare the word lists and discuss them. Why do certain words affect individuals as they do? How were the words acquired and do their meanings, as understood by the students, have a basis of fact?

33. Tape-record a short radio newscast that presents facts without commentary. Also record a news commentator who broadcasts his own opinions among the facts. Play the two recordings before the class. Ask the students to point out the differences between the two recordings. Can the students separate fact from opinion in the news commentary?

34. After they hear a classroom talk on some subject such as geography or biology, ask the students to plan a film strip that might be used to illustrate the oral material.

35. Record a number of radio advertisements, or select several from magazines to read aloud before the class. When selecting the advertisements, look for ones using specific propaganda techniques (see Chapter 11). Ex-

plain the propaganda techniques to the class and then have the students listen to the advertisements. As they listen, can they identify the propaganda techniques?

36. As part of any training in public speaking, include listening criticism as well as criticism of speeches. When a student completes a talk, ask him to comment on his classmates' listening. Was he distracted by anyone in the audience? Why? Did the attention of his student audience vary from point to point in his speech?

37. Explain to the class how a formal speech is organized (see Chapter 6). Find or compose a speech that is carefully organized. Tape-record the speech, leaving thirty-second pauses at each main point of partitioning of the talk. Play it back to the class. During each pause, identify the part of the speech just completed and the one that will be heard in a few seconds. Record another such speech, but with no pauses, and ask the students to identify the different parts of the talk. If no tape recorder is available, this exercise can be practiced with the teacher reading the speeches aloud.

38. Obtain several spoken-word records of literature and play them to the class. After each record is heard, discuss meanings that the students might have obtained from the records by "listening between the lines." (See Chapter 7.) In other words, ask the students to listen for meaning that was not put into words on the recording.

39. Around a premise that the students might strongly favor (perhaps one for longer vacations) compose a five-minute speech with one-sided evidence supporting the premise. Deliberately leave out evidence that does not support it. Read the speech to the class and ask them to criticize it *objectively*. Were the speech's ideas supported

soundly? Would the students want to hear more evidence before reaching a decision on the subject? How would the talk affect someone who was not in favor of the premise presented?

40. Explain the two listening concentration skills of mentally summarizing and anticipating what we hear (see Chapter 7). Read a short speech aloud to the class. At a point, perhaps three-quarters of the way through the speech, stop talking. Ask the students first to write a short summary of what they heard, and then a brief statement of what they were anticipating in the speech. When the writing is completed, read the entire speech through, allowing the students to check their abilities at summarizing and anticipating.

41. Send six students (we'll label them A through F for purposes of explanation) out of the room. Read a short, dramatic passage from a story to the remaining class members. Call student A back into the room. Ask him to listen carefully as a classmate (one who remained in the room) repeats the story that was read. Then ask student A to relay the story to student B as he enters the room. Following the same procedure, B tells C, C tells D, D tells E and E tells F. Student F finishes the relay by reporting what he heard to the class. Tape-record each version of the story, including the one that was read aloud. After the exercise is complete, play back the entire recording. Did the story change as it passed from student to student? If so, what caused the changes? Discuss the project, giving special attention to how emotions can actually change what we hear (see Chapter 8). Repeat the experiment in an effort to make the repetition more accurate.

42. When an assignment of student speeches has been made for a class hour, inform the group that after each talk one of the listeners will be asked by random choice to arise and give a two-minute critique of his classmate's effort. The critique should focus upon the content and organization of the speech given rather than upon the delivery techniques of the speaker. All critiques are graded with the same importance as are the original talks.

43. After considerable practice with the above procedure, use the same routine except that the student critic must criticize the next-to-the-last talk given (the first two talks are given without interruption for critiques).

44. As still greater skill in listening is achieved, repeat the above routine, but with each critic required to criticize a talk after which there have been two intervening speeches (the first three speeches are given without any interruption for critiques).

The foregoing suggestions, which certainly do not include all of the possibilities for listening instruction, may prime a flow of ideas among teachers that can lead to more and better methods of teaching the subject.

FOR IMPROVED LEARNING, GROWTH, AND UNDERSTANDING

In this age of the spoken word, it is no longer wise to allow our children to proceed through school with little or no formal attention to listening. In view of the need for it, our educators, in the not too distant future, are certain to find ways of including listening training in their curriculums.

In years ahead more and more of us will have the opportunity to sharpen our listening abilities while receiving guidance from experts in this field. It seems that we shall eventually come to believe that the responsibility for effective oral communication must be equally shared by speakers and listeners. When this transpires we shall have taken a long stride toward greater economy in learning, accelerated personal growth, and significantly deepened human understanding.

Selected Bibliography

Sources drawn upon in preparing this book, plus suggested reading on the subject of *listening:*

Allport, Gordon W., and Leo Postman, *The Psychology of Rumor,* Henry Holt and Company, Inc., New York, 1948.

Anderson, Harold A., "Teaching the Art of Listening," *School Review,* lvii (February, 1949), pp. 63–67.

Baird, A. Craig, and Franklin H. Knower, *General Speech,* McGraw-Hill Book Company, Inc., New York, 1949.

Berelson, Bernard R., Paul F. Lazarsfeld, and William N. Mc-Phee, *Voting,* The University of Chicago Press, 1954.

Bird, Donald E., "Have You Tried Listening?" *Journal of the American Dietetic Association* (March, 1954), pp. 225–230.

Blewett, Thomas T., "An Experiment in the Measurement of Listening at the College Level," Unpublished doctor's dissertation, University of Missouri, 1945.

Borchers, Gladys, "An Approach to the Problem of Oral Style," *Quarterly Journal of Speech,* vol. 22 (February, 1936).

Brewster, Lawrence W., "An Exploratory Study of Some Aspects of Critical Listening among College Freshmen," Unpublished doctor's thesis, State University of Iowa, June, 1956.

Brown, James Isaac: "The Construction of a Diagnostic Test of Listening Comprehension," Uupublished doctor's dissertation, University of Colorado, 1949.

Cantril, Hadley, *Invasion from Mars,* Princeton University Press, 1940.

Dooher, M. Joseph and Vivienne Marquis, *Effective Communication on the Job,* American Management Association, New York, 1956.

English Language Arts, Prepared by the Commission on English Curriculum of the National Council of Teachers of

English, Appleton-Century-Crofts, Inc., New York, 1952.

Freed, Conrad W., "Silent Conditioning in the Schools," *Quarterly Journal of Speech,* xxvii (April, 1941), pp. 188–194.

Gardner, Erle Stanley, "How to Know You're Transparent When You'd Like to Be Opaque," *Vogue* (July, 1956), pp. 45–47.

Goldstein, Harry, "Reading and Listening Comprehension at Various Controlled Rates," *Contributions to Education,* No. 821, Bureau of Publications, Teachers College, Columbia University, 1940.

Hamilton, Mrs. Ruth Hewitt, " 'From Drawbridge to Castle'— Stories Reign Supreme," *Junior Libraries,* vol. 3 (September, 1956).

Haugh, Oscar M., "The Comparative Value of Reading and Listening in the Acquisition of Information and the Changing of Attitudes," Unpublished doctor's thesis, University of Minnesota, 1950.

Hayakawa, S. I., "How to Attend a Conference," *ETC.,* xiii (Autumn, 1955), pp. 5–9.

Heilman, Arthur, "Measuring and Improving Listening Ability," Unpublished doctor's thesis, University of Iowa, 1950.

Heye, Helen, "A Study of the Effectiveness of Selected Auditory Presentations at the Adult Level," Unpublished doctor's thesis, University of Iowa, 1941.

Irvin, Charles E., "Conclusions about Listening Habits of Freshmen at Michigan State College," Unpublished typed manuscript reporting three exploratory studies made over a period of two years.

Johnson, Wendell, "Do You Know How to Listen?" *ETC.,* xii (Autumn, 1949).

Katz, Elihu, and Paul F. Lazarsfeld, *Personal Influence,* The Free Press, Glencoe, Illinois, 1955.

Knower, Franklin N. S., David Phillips, and Fern Koeppel, "Studies in Listening to Informative Speaking," *Journal of Abnormal and Social Psychology,* vol. 40 (February, 1945), pp. 82–88.

Krawier, Theophile, "A Comparison of Learning and Retention of Materials Presented Visually and Auditorially," Unpublished doctor's thesis, New York University, 1945.

Lazarsfeld, Paul F., Bernard Berelson, and Hazel Gaudet, *The People's Choice*, Columbia University Press, 1948.

Lazarsfeld, Paul F., and Frank N. Stanton, "What Do We Really Know About Day-time Serial Listeners?" by Herta Herzog; and "The World of the Day-time Serial," by Rudolf Arnheim; *Radio Research*, 1942–1943, Duell, Sloan & Pearce, Inc., New York.

Lee, Irving J., *How to Talk with People*, Harper & Brothers, New York, 1952.

Mercer, Jessie, "Listening in the Speech Class," *The Bulletin of the National Association of Secondary School Principals*, vol. 32 (January, 1948), pp. 102–107.

Mersand, Joseph, "Why Teach Listening?," Paper read at the Fortieth Annual Meeting of the National Council of Teachers of English, Milwaukee, 1950.

Morkovin, Boris V., "Growth through Speaking and Listening," *Elementary English*, xxvi (March, 1949), pp. 127–128, 157.

Nichols, Ralph G., "Factors Accounting for Differences in Comprehension of Materials Presented Orally in the Classroom," Unpublished doctor's dissertation, State University of Iowa, 1948.

Nichols, Ralph G., "Listening Instruction in the Secondary School," Special Bulletin of the National Association of Secondary School Principals," Article 14, 1951.

Nichols, Ralph G., and Thomas R. Lewis, *Listening and Speaking*, Wm. C. Brown Company, Dubuque, Iowa, 1954.

Nichols, Ralph G., and Leonard A. Stevens, "You Don't Know How to Listen," *Collier's* (July 25, 1953).

Phifer, Gregg, "Propaganda and Critical Listening," *Journal of Communication*, May, 1953.

Rankin, Paul T., "Listening Ability," Proceedings of the Ohio State Educational Conference, pp. 172–183, Ohio State University, Columbus, 1939.

Reik, Theodor, *Listening with the Third Ear,* Farrar, Straus & Co., New York, 1949.

Ribble, Margaret A., "The Self Emerges," *Wisdom* (April, 1956), p. 27.

Rogers, Carl R., and R. J. Roethlisberger, "Barriers and Gateways to Communication," *Harvard Business Review,* xxx, No. 4 (July–August, 1952).

Sayers, Francis Clarke, "From Me to You," *Junior Libraries,* vol. 3 (September, 1956).

Stevens, Leonard A., *A Comparison of Reading and Listening Comprehension of News Writing,* Unpublished master's thesis, State University of Iowa, 1949.

Whyte, William H. Jr., *"Is Anybody Listening?,"* Simon and Schuster, Inc., New York, 1952.

Wiksell, W. A., "Problems of Listening," *Quarterly Journal of Speech,* xxxii (December, 1946), pp. 505–508.

Wilt, Miriam E., "What Is the Listening Ration in Your Classroom?," *Elementary English,* xxvi (May, 1949), pp. 259–264.

Wilt, Miriam E., "A Study of Teacher Awareness of Listening as a Factor in Elementary Education," Unpublished doctor's dissertation, Pennsylvania State College, 1949.

Index

227

233

About the Authors

Dr. Ralph G. Nichols is Professor of Speech and Chairman of the Department of Rhetoric at the University of Minnesota. He is widely known as a pioneer in the field of listening efficiency and for the past six years has served as Chairman of a National Committee on Listening Comprehension. Dr. Nichols has been President of the National Society for the Study of Communication and of the Iowa State and Minnesota State Speech Teachers Association. His experience, study and research in the field of listening have led to training programs in industry, government, education and the military service. He is the author of many published articles and of a widely used textbook, *Listening and Speaking*.

Leonard A. Stevens is a free-lance magazine writer and also does consulting work in industrial communications. While studying for his Bachelor's and Master's degrees at the University of Iowa he became interested in the subject of listening. It was at this time that he met Professor Nichols, who was doing his first research in that field. Mr. Stevens' interest in communication took him into radio news broadcasting and then as a speaker for the Citizens' Committee for the Hoover Report. Mr. Stevens' magazine articles have appeared in *The Saturday Evening Post, Reader's Digest, McCall's,* and many other magazines.

Both authors lecture extensively on the subject of listening.